The Complete Credit Care™ Program

Stan Morris

THE COMPLETE CREDIT CARE ™ PROGRAM
Copyright © 2021 by Stan Morris

All rights reserved. No part of this publication may be reproduced, distributed, or transmitted in any form or by any means, including photocopying, recording, or other electronic or mechanical methods, without the prior written permission of the publisher or author, except in the case of brief quotations embodied in critical reviews and certain other noncommercial uses permitted by copyright law.

Although every precaution has been taken to verify the accuracy of the information contained herein, the author and publisher assume no responsibility for any errors or omissions. No liability is assumed for damages that may result from the use of information contained within.

Library of Congress Control Number: 2021912292
ISBN-13: Paperback: 978-1-64749-507-7
Epub: 978-1-64749-508-4

Printed in the United States of America

GoTo Publish

GoToPublish LLC
1-888-337-1724
www.gotopublish.com
info@gotopublish.com

So You Want to Improve Your Credit.

"The Complete CreditCare™ Program" is designed to help everyone understand the credit reporting process.

- Learn why credit bureaus make it hard for individuals to improve credit scores
- Learn a way to receive free credit reports
- Learn how to recognize and dispute errors to improve your credit score
- Learn what it takes to remove damaging errors from your report
- Learn how to build a good credit score even if you've never had credit
- Learn the Federal Credit Report Act so no one can ever take advantage of you
- Track your progress with an easy to understand planner

By Stan Morris
Credit Repair Specialist

"***The Complete CreditCare™ Program***" Is dedicated to my wife Lisa and children, Shawn & Stacy, Mandy & Jason and Caleb. A special thanks to Bert Lewis for proofing and editing this book. It's also dedicated to everyone who has gone through hard financial times and wants to improve his or her quality of life by levelling the playing field. I want to offer another special thanks to Char and Harry Anzalone. No matter how difficult things became, they we always there telling me "you can do it."

Table Of Contents

Reasons to Improve Your Credit Score.................................6

How much Is Bad Credit Costing You?.............................8

Overall Plan..10

FCRA Summary..14

Learn To Read A Credit Report...16

CRA Phone Numbers...55

The Two Fold Approach Plan..57

Let's Get Started..58

Disputing Creditors Directly 61

Incorrect Payment History...62

P&L and Charge-Off Accounts...63

Debt Collectors..64

Another Methods To Remove Errors 65

Add Some Good Credit..66

What If You've Never Had Any Credit?.............................68

Build Credit Using Current Bills..69

Secured Credit cards..70

Sample Letters..72-114

Credit Care "Tracking Your Success"..........................115-139

STAN MORRIS

Note From The Author

Every part of our life is touched by credit. I've found out in the past few years it's hard to do much without a good credit score. Having an excellent credit score is even better. Many people don't know or understand how credit scores are calculated or anything much about credit scores. I can tell you this. Credit Reporting Agencies are tied to big lenders and lenders are tied to lobbyists and lobbyists are tied to law makers. This is a lethal combination for consumers' financial health. Credit Reporting Agencies can report items that are not accurate. It's up to you, the consumer, to get them corrected. It has been estimated that over 75% of Americans have errors on their reports. America's average credit score is under 700. In my opinion the industry is set up to protect the lenders and not the consumer. This results in billions of unwarranted dollars spent on interest to lenders. I'll prove that many people, maybe even you, pay too much for borrowing money for federally mandated insurances. Let me say that your local lenders are not the cause of this. They are required to be part of it but not the cause. This book is designed to give you an overview. It will teach you how to level the playing field when dealing with collection agencies and other entities that place derogatory information on your report. Just keep in mind that CRAs are not for you, the consumer. They make money because of you. If they can keep you in a credit range of 540-680 they will make more money than someone with an 800 score. I could have put other things in this book. I included the things I thought were most important in helping someone improve his or her credit score.

THE COMPLETE CREDIT CARE™ PROGRAM

Reasons To Improve Your Credit Score

Today just about everything we pay for is tied to a credit score. If your credit score is low then expect to pay more for most goods and services. Car loans and insurance for your car is just a couple of things that will cost you more if you have a low credit score. I'm talking about a significantly higher amount if your score is below 620. In fact just these two costs together could cost you more than $200.00 a month more than someone with a 720 score. As time goes on and lenders, insurance giants and other businesses figure out more ways to justify charging people more for their goods and services, other important things like health insurance, food, etc. will be higher as well. I know this sounds a little far-fetched so I want you to think ahead with me and look into a future possible scenario. Let's imagine it's 2020 and you and your wife want to order pizza. She calls the local pizza parlor and the conversation goes like this.

Generations' Pizza How can I help you?

I want to order a pizza delivered to my home at 1234 Main Street, please.

Ok what's your phone number?

It's 870-598-1111.

Ok, Mrs. Morris. Can I have your social security number?

Yes. It's 1111-11-1111.

Ok what kind of Pizza can I get for you?

I want a large supreme with thick crust.

Ok, Mrs. Morris there will be a $7.00 surcharge because I see that Mr. Morris has high cholesterol and isn't supposed to eat this kind of pizza. Will you be paying with a credit card, check or cash today?

I'll be writing a check. What's the total?

It'll be an extra $10.00 Mrs. Morris because your credit score is below 620. If you pay cash I can knock that off.

I know this sounds unfathomable and probably will never happen. I just wanted to call attention to how much our society has changed in the last 20 years and how much it could change in the next ten. More and more industries will figure out how to cash in on the credit score fiasco. That's why everyone should know exactly what their credit score is. Everyone should monitor his score at least once a year and clean up anything that is negative. If you will take the time to learn about this important part of your life then I can assure you that you will save thousands and thousands of dollars over your life time. The American Dream has been tainted by American Greed.

THE COMPLETE CREDIT CARE ™ PROGRAM

How Much Is a Bad Credit Score Costing You?

If your score is below whatever the lenders consider good credit then you are paying a premium for the privilege to use their money. Lenders have worked out a formula where they can risk money based on the assumption they will have a certain percentage of customers default on loans that have low credit scores. This is called sub-prime lending. Let's say in our example we view 100 customers. Out of those 100 customers the lender knows how many of those people will default on their loans. So they can adjust the interest rate to capture enough from all the other subprime borrowers to cover their loss on the ones that actually default. It's a little more complicated but this is one of the factors of why subprime loans cost more. That personally affects you if you have bad credit. Over the period of 30 years a person with bad credit could very well spend an extra $500,000 or more in extra interest payments or higher insurance premiums and services such as phones. I'll prove it to you later in this program.

Here are items for which you already pay higher fees if you have bad credit.

Auto loan: National Automobile Dealers Association: Claims the average car loan is almost $25,000. Just think. An auto loan for a person with good credit would carry a 7% APR, while someone with bad credit (620 or below) would have to pay a 17%-21% APR. This works out to a difference of $95 or more a month, which comes to $3,400 over the three years of the loan. The average person keeps their car for 4 years.

This means if each person financed a new car every four years, it would cost the person with bad credit $27,000 or more in car financing over 32 years than someone with good credit.

Mortgage: Another purchase in which bad credit hurts you is the interest rate you must pay when you purchase a house. The average price for a home in June 2009 was $250,000.

A 30-year, $200,000 loan for someone with a Excellent credit score carried a 6.346% APR. Others with lower credit scores of around 620 would have a 9.5% APR. This means a person with a good score would have a monthly payment of $1,118, while the person with the bad credit score would pay $1,687 or $569.00 a month more for the same house. That adds up to $204,840.00 over the 30 years of the loan.

Job: More and more employers are checking your credit. I had a relative that applied at a national floral supply company a few years ago. They didn't hire her because of a previous bankruptcy. This person actually helped run a multimillion dollar business and would have made this national company a lot of money because of her experience.

Credit cards: Let's assume, for example, that the people with good and bad credit both carry a median credit card debt of $2,200 over 30 years. If the person with good credit had an interest rate of 8% and the person with bad credit had an interest rate of 28%, the person with bad credit will pay an extra $9,850 over a 30 year period.

Insurance: Just about any insurance you pay for like auto, homeowners, and life will probably cost more for a person with bad credit than one with good credit. Insurance companies try to charge more because they say families with bad credit make more claims than those with good credit. I think this is false. We are supposed to have government agencies watching out for this sort of extortion but in my opinion they aren't doing a very good job. What independent study was done? Who paid for it, even if it were actually performed?

Housing: Most apartment managers will run a credit check on prospective tenants. If your credit is poor, you may not be able to rent because the manager might think you won't pay because of your past credit history.

Deposits: There are many companies that won't let you purchase their services without large deposits. Cell phone companies are a good example of this. Other businesses like utilities, apartment rentals, etc. can also charge more deposit before they will provide goods or services.

Here's an answer to "how much is low credit costing Americans?" Auto $95 month, House $569 month, Lower paying job $1000.00 month, Credit cards $50.00, Insurance premiums $100.00 a month. The total extra cost in this scenario is **$1800.00 per month**. That totals **$21,768**.00 a year and **$653,040.00** over a **lifetime**. These are estimates and you may not be paying this much extra, however one of your categories may be higher and some a little less. All in all, if you have low credit scores, you are paying more for most of the things you buy and that are the facts. I challenge you to take inventory of your personal situation and see where you can improve your standard of living by improving your credit score instead of paying more than you deserve to pay by having a low credit score. Please do not start trying to pay cash for everything you purchase. That will end up costing you more for the things like insurance etc. Learn to use credit to benefit you.

THE COMPLETE CREDIT CARE ™ PROGRAM

An Overall Plan Must Be Laid To Be Successful Improving Your Credit Score.

Over the years I've learned firsthand that in order to increase your credit score you must have a plan. The most successful plan I've used for several of my clients has been the following. 1) Find and dispute all the items on the three bureaus reports that are inaccurate, incomplete or unverifiable. 2) Create new accounts that show you can manage your financial affairs. These two methods will improve your score and will change your life. It depends where you start. (What your score is and what is causing your score to be what it is, as to how long it will take to raise it enough to improve your standard of living.)

Here are some things you must know in order to improve your score.

1) What is the score I need to be able to pay a fair amount of interest for the things I purchase?
(A) 720. You can get some things at an increased rate presently at a 620-630. I know of a recent loan for a $51,000.00 new truck for a customer of mine where the interest was 6.99%. I expect interest rates to increase over the next year or so as America (and the world) start dealing with deficits. That makes it even more important for your scores to improve over the next few months. History has shown as the money supply tightens the folks with the best interest rates will be able to borrow money and the folks with poor credit won't be able to borrow anything.

(2) What is a credit score?
(A) A credit score is a complicated number that is derived by the Fair Isaacs Company. The Fair Isaacs Company uses an algorithm that takes all your past and present credit history and composes a numeric value that lenders and other big businesses use to determine your credit worthiness or your risk factor. This numeric figure can range from 0 to 850. 0-619 is POOR and 620-719 LENDABLE. One can buy things but might pay higher interest. 720-850 is EXCELLENT. Here is where one pays the best amount of interest. The interesting thing about all this is lenders can change their model that they will lend toward at any given time. In other words you may not be able to get a loan today because you have a low credit score of maybe 619. Tomorrow that same lender might need a loan to finish out a particular goal and lend you the money. Another reason this changes is the money supply. If money is tight your loan may not even be considered today and in two months it might fall into the scope of their lending criteria. A good example of this is when the housing market crashed in 2008. Automobile lenders tightened their belts and it was difficult to get any loans approved without money down and a score of 680-720 and above. At the time of this writing I've seen loans for scores less than 600 and no money down. In the near future I believe things will tighten up for a few years. This makes it more important for a person to get their financial house in order. If you are in the vicious credit crunch cycle then it's time to get out of credit prison before the door is slammed and not opened for a while. I think it's time to make a statement that may surprise you. You do not have to have a lot of money to have a good quality life. You do have to have good credit. Just learn to manage what you have coming in. It's just like

having two boxes. Imagine one box is all the money coming in and the other box represents all the money you spend. The goal is to have some left at the end of every week in the box where you put the money that comes in. Do whatever it takes to accomplish that and your quality of life will be better than if you don't do that. One of the ways to have more left in the income box is pay less for goods and services. In other words if you cut your insurance costs because you've increased your credit score then you'll have more left at week's end. Another way to increase the amount left in the income box is to decrease your car payment by improving your credit score. If you cut your payment by $75.00 a month you've just saved almost $900 a year. If you're paying a tote your note lot for your car I assure you you're paying alot for what you're getting because most tote your note lots will not report to the credit bureaus. I understand that it's better than nothing but when you get your credit up you might pay a monthly payment in the amount that you pay every month just to maintain the car you're driving now.

3) Who are the credit Bureaus?

(A) There are three main ones.

    1). Transunion

    2). Equifax

    3). Experian

Each bureau collects information about you and most Americans. The bureaus have exploded with the advent of computers because they can obtain and use the information in so many different ways. Bureaus sell your credit history to lenders, insurance companies, credit cards companies, and retail businesses like car lots, furniture stores or anyone else that will pay for this information. Most of us have received pre-approval letters from credit card companies and car dealers before. This is just a small example of how your information is sold. Your information has been collected by the companies you have done business within the past and present. These companies send information regarding your credit to the bureaus. They send information like, when you borrowed the money, how much, the date, your credit limit (in the case of credit cards) and every month how well you service the debt. They report if the account is open or closed and if you're late how many times and how often. They report if it is charged off, in bankruptcy or sold to another lender. It's a funny thing. I have never seen where a mistake has been made by the bureaus whereby a person has been reported twice for a positive account from a lender that was a mistake. I have seen several adverse accounts reported on one bureau report that was negative. This information is collected from companies that you do business with and they are called furnishers. There are other furnishers as well. They collect information from your local, state and federal court systems. These companies collect information for judgments, bankruptcy, felonies etc. The bureaus are called CRAs. This stands for credit reporting agencies. There is a fourth CRA called Innovis. It supplies information for your pre-approval credit cards . Presently they get their information from the other bureaus but they are growing and soon, if not already there will be a fourth CRA that will have to be reckoned with. So at present there are 5 major players who have your private information, FICO, Transunion, Equifax, Experian and Innovis. As you are trying to improve your scores the main three you'll be dealing with is TransUnion, Equifax and Experian. One product all three companies sell is for car dealers. It's important to note that the score the CRA report to you could be different than ones car dealers get. The reason for this is that the car industry has a scoring model that's different from the plain old score they give you. In other words when a car dealer buys a report from Transunion it is industry specific for the automobile industry. An example of this, I've noticed, is more points taken off your credit score if you've had a previous repo than is taken off your generic report from the same CRA. Is it fair? No. It's just another way for lenders to get more interest from you. And that brings up another point that I need to cover now. CRAs are for-profit companies. They are huge companies that make millions and millions of profit dollars every year. They are no different than your company or the company that you work for. They sell products called information. The information is free to them.

CRAs are fallible. They make mistakes. In fact it has been proven that 75%-80% of the credit reports contain errors in the form of items that are old and out dated, items that are not provable, items that are inaccurate and items that are incomplete. They make these reports so hard to understand that the average American takes what they see on their report as gospel and can't fix their credit because they don't understand what they are looking at. Sometimes it's not what's on the report but what's not on the report. It's important for CRAs to have your credit score as low as possible. The reason is because lower scores are more valuable to them. This gives them leverage to sell their products. If a bank doesn't use their CRA scoring system then they may be out of compliance with the federal regulations. If they are out of compliance then they may go out of business. Another reason is CRAs; say to lenders "You need this report because what if you sell to a person who doesn't pay his or her bills?" Low scores give CRAs leverage. If everyone's score was excellent then there would be no need for them. Another very important reason the CRAs want you to have a lower score is their customers (Lenders, Insurance Companies, etc.) can make more money from lower scored customers by charging more in interest or in insurance cases, higher premiums. So, by that, I want you to know how I view CRAs and too big to fail corporations. They have too much power over our lives. They are not required to make sure that the items on your credit report are accurate before they report it. They can report anything on your report that a furnisher reports to them without ever verifying the item to be accurate beforehand. These companies make more money if your credit report is low because they can sell your data more often to different companies. In other words companies want to market to lower scored individuals so these individuals are sought after. So if powerful companies like CRAs have the ability to slant our score lower, they can make more money. Believe me it will happen. In fact it is happening right now. I believe the credit report is a document filled with allegations. I live in America and I believe in "innocent until proven guilty." By this I believe that each negative item must be viewed as an allegation and must be proven accurate, complete and "properly verified" before I will accept it as a viable instrument to use as a scoring tool that dictates my quality of life. The US Federal Government believes the same thing because they passed laws a few years ago that state the same thing. It's called the FCRA. This law is being used by people like you and me every day to improve their credit scores. I might add here that the CRAs make it as difficult as they can on everyday Americans when it comes to using our rights to clean up erroneous problems on what they are reporting. They hire lots of people to handle all the disputes that roll in. These extra people cost them lots of money and CRAs don't like credit score increases because it costs them in many other ways.

THE COMPLETE CREDIT CARE ™ PROGRAM

A Summary Of Your Rights Under The Fair Credit Reporting Act

The federal Fair Credit Reporting Act (FCRA) promotes the accuracy, fairness, and privacy of information in the files of consumer reporting agencies. There are many types of consumer reporting agencies, including credit bureaus and specialty agencies (such as agencies that sell information about check writing histories, medical records, and rental history records). Here is a summary of your major rights under the FCRA. **For more information, including information about additional rights, go to www.ftc.gov/credit or write to: Consumer Response Center, Room 130-A, Federal Trade Commission, 600 Pennsylvania Ave. N.W., Washington, D.C. 20580.**

- **You must be told if information in your file has been used against you.** Anyone who uses a credit report or another type of consumer report to deny your application for credit, insurance, or employment – or to take another adverse action against you – must tell you, and must give you the name, address, and phone number of the agency that provided the information.
- **You have the right to know what is in your file.** You may request and obtain all the information about you in the files of a consumer reporting agency (your "file disclosure"). You will be required to provide proper identification, which may include your Social Security number. In many cases, the disclosure will be free. You are entitled to a free file disclosure if:
o a person has taken adverse action against you because of information in your credit report;
o you are the victim of identify theft and place a fraud alert in your file;
o your file contains inaccurate information as a result of fraud;
o you are on public assistance;
o you are unemployed but expect to apply for employment within 60 days.
In addition, by September 2005 all consumers will be entitled to one free disclosure every 12 months upon request from each nationwide credit bureau and from nationwide specialty consumer reporting agencies. See www.ftc.gov/credit for additional information.
- **You have the right to ask for a credit score.** Credit scores are numerical summaries of your credit-worthiness based on information from credit bureaus. You may request a credit score from consumer reporting agencies that create scores or distribute scores used in residential real property loans, but you will have to pay for it. In some mortgage transactions, you will receive credit score information for free from the mortgage lender.
- **You have the right to dispute incomplete or inaccurate information.** If you identify information in your file that is incomplete or inaccurate, and report it to the consumer reporting agency, the agency must investigate unless your dispute is frivolous. See www.ftc.gov/credit for an explanation of dispute procedures.
- **Consumer reporting agencies must correct or delete inaccurate, incomplete, or unverifiable information.** Inaccurate, incomplete or unverifiable information must be removed or corrected, usually within 30 days. However, a consumer reporting agency may continue to report information it has verified as accurate.
- **Consumer reporting agencies may not report outdated negative information.** In most cases, a consumer reporting agency may not report negative information that is more than seven years old, or
bankruptcies that are more than 10 years old. 122.103.29 FCRA Summary of Rights 7/18/2009
- **Access to your file is limited.** A consumer reporting agency may provide information about you only to people with a valid need -- usually to consider an application with a creditor, insurer, employer, landlord, or other business. The FCRA specifies those with a valid need for access.
- **You must give your consent for reports to be provided to employers.** A consumer reporting agency may not give out information about you to your employer, or a potential employer, without your written consent given to the employer. Written consent generally is not required in the trucking industry. For more information, go to www.ftc.gov/credit.
- **You may limit "prescreened" offers of credit and insurance you get based on information in your credit report.** Unsolicited "prescreened" offers for credit and insurance must include a toll-free phone number you can call if you choose to remove your

name and address from the lists these offers are based on. You may opt-out with the nationwide credit bureaus at 1-888-5-OPTOUT (1-888-567-8688).
• **You may seek damages from violators.** If a consumer reporting agency, or, in some cases, a user of consumer reports or a furnisher of information to a consumer reporting agency violates the FCRA, you may be able to sue in state or federal court.
• **Identity theft victims and active duty military personnel have additional rights.** For more information, visit www.ftc.gov/credit.
States may enforce the FCRA, and many states have their own consumer reporting laws. In some cases, you may have more rights under state law. For more information, contact your state or local consumer protection agency or your state Attorney General.

Below are the websites for each bureau. If you want to read the entire FCRA law then go to www.ftc.gov/credit . You can also go to your state and Google state credit reporting laws. Each states laws is similar. There are slight differences. Another Federal law that would be worth reading is The Federal law that regulates collection. You should also Google State Collection Laws for (your state). For the purpose of this book the FCRA included above will suffice.

C Equifax: ; www.equifax.com
C Experian: ; www.experian.com
C TransUnion: www.transunion.com

THE COMPLETE CREDIT CARE™ PROGRAM

Pull Your Credit Report And Learn To Read It.

Attacking the low credit score problem in two ways should make a little more sense now that you understand more about how credit bureaus work. So the first thing we must do is grab a credit report and start looking at things that have brought your score down so much. The second step is once these most adverse items have been identified is to dispute them. Dispute them if they are outdated, inaccurate, not verifiable, or if you don't recognize them. Once they are disputed and sent off we must deal with the results of the investigations by the bureaus. You'll get some of them off but not all the first round. It may take several disputes to get enough items off your report to increase your score enough to make a difference. During this process get a couple of credit cards. If you can't get any issued then go to some secured credit cards and get one of those. Believe me it is better than nothing. If you use it properly the company will issue a card that will do even more to improve your credit. This effort may take 2 months and it may take longer. It depends on where you are starting from and what has caused your score to be low.

Let's get started by pulling the credit report.

I like to use www.freecreditchecktotal.com this is a site that Experian owns. You simply fill in the information they request and you get all three reports with scores. You have to give them a credit card number. If you don't want to keep using the service then you have to call the toll free number and cancel the free trail. You have 7 days to do this. Otherwise they are going to charge you from $19-$21 a month for the reports. If you have the money and it won't put you in a financial bind I recommend using this monthly service while you are repairing your credit. If you decide to opt out here is the toll free number to call. 1-866-506-7894

Example Report:

Personal Profile			
Here you will find the personal information contained in your credit file, including your legal name(s), address(es), current and previous employers, and date of birth.			
	EXPERIAN	EQUIFAX	TRANSUNION
Name:	Joe Blow	Joe Blow	Joe Blow
Also Known As:			
Year of Birth:	1977	1977	1977
Address(es):	1708 COUNTY ROAD 608, Somewhere, St 63xxx	1708 COUNTY ROAD 608, Somewhere, St 63xxx	1708 COUNTY ROAD 608, Somewhere, St 63xxx
	1xx COUNTY ROAD xxx, Somewhere, ST 63xxx	1xx COUNTY ROAD xxx, Somewhere, ST 63xxx	1xx COUNTY ROAD xxx, Somewhere, ST 63xxx
	923 APPLE ST, Somewhere else 63xxxx	923 APPLE ST, Somewhere else 63xxxx	923 APPLE ST, Somewhere else 63xxxx
Current Employer:	Good Company	Good Company	Good Company
Previous Employer(s):	MORKIN	MORKIN	MORKIN

The above section is where your personal information is reported. Make sure the addresses and State are correct. If you see a wrong address, write a letter to the bureaus and have them correct the error. If there is a wrong state it is very possible there is identity theft going on. You'll know more as you look through the rest of your report. If you find there is fraud or identity theft call one of the bureaus and they will put a fraud alert on your file and contact the other bureaus and they will do the same.

Credit Summary

This section gives you a broad look at your current and past credit status. Here you'll find the total number of open and closed accounts in your name, the total balance on those accounts, and delinquencies.

	EXPERIAN	EQUIFAX	TRANSUNION
REAL ESTATE ACCOUNTS:			
Count	0	0	1
Balance	$0.00	$0.00	$41,759.00
Current	0	0	1
Delinquent	0	0	0
Other	0	0	0
REVOLVING ACCOUNTS:			
Count	3	3	3
Balance	$7.00	$7.00	$7.00
Current	1	1	1
Delinquent	0	0	0
Other	1	0	0
INSTALLMENT ACCOUNTS:			
Count	10	2	8
Balance	$4,935.00	$2,126.00	$13,636.00
Current	1	1	7
Delinquent	1	1	0
Other	1	0	0
OTHER ACCOUNTS:			
Count	0	16	3
Balance	$0.00	$3,707.00	$9,662.00
Current	0	7	3
Delinquent	0	9	0
Other	0	0	0
COLLECTION ACCOUNTS:			
Count	7	7	15
Balance	$2,074.00	$1,477.00	$5,230.00
Current	1	1	0
Delinquent	0	0	0
Other	0	0	0
TOTAL ACCOUNTS:			
Count	20	28	30
Balance	$7,016.00	$7,317.00	$70,294.00
Current	3	10	12
Delinquent	1	10	0
Other	2	0	0
ACCOUNTS SUMMARY:			
Open Accounts:	2	0	22
Closed Accounts:	18	0	8
Public Records:	1	0	0
Inquiries:	6	15	27

The credit summary is just that. It shows what credit amounts are reporting at each bureau. Each Bureau reports items in different categories. Real Estate, Revolving (Credit Cards, etc), Installments (Auto, etc), other and then collections. Look at each bureau and category closely. Compare the totals in each category. There may be some bureaus not reporting some of your positive accounts. If that's the case, look through the reports history section, find the accounts and ask the bureaus that's not reporting positive accounts, to report them. There are examples of this throughout the CrreditCare™ program. The example report has a

THE COMPLETE CREDIT CARE ™ PROGRAM

lot of discrepancy between the bureaus and accounts. Transunion is reporting much more. Notice, Transunion is reporting a mortgage and more installments than Equifax and Experian. For instance, Equifax and Tranunion aren't reporting the home loan. If you have a similar situation and your loan is current and will help bring your score up, ask the other bureaus to report it. If you've been late within the past two years then it still may be worth having the other bureaus report it. If you are 60 days late presently don't bother. Wait until it turns back positive and then get it reported. Notice the collection accounts next. There are several more on Transunion than the other CRA'S are reporting. It would be important to find those and start working on them first. Anything that is younger than 2 years old is the ones we want to dispute first. TransUnion is the bureau that most car dealerships use to check your credit. When you're applying for a home loan all three bureaus are used. The high score and low score is discarded and the middle score is used. In other words, if you had a score with Experian of 580, a score with Equifax of 620 and a score with Transunion of 680, the score that the lenders would use is 620. It's important to fix all three.

Public Records

The information in this section comes from federal district bankruptcy records, state and county court records, tax liens and monetary judgments, and in some states, overdue child support records. Public records remain on your credit report for 7-10 years.

	EXPERIAN	EQUIFAX	TRANSUNION
Type:	Judgment satisfied		Bankruptcy
Date Filed:	1/23/2008		Released 1/1/2004
Reference #:	084TCV0		Fed Court 1xx34
Court:	A CNTY ASSOC CT		
Plaintiff:	MTS ACCEPTANCE INC		
Liability:	$2934.00		$0
Asset:			

^Top of Page^

Public Records is where you'll find things like judgments and bankruptcies. Look the dates over well. If they aren't accurate or if they aren't yours or if they've been on there for more than 7 years you can challenge them and many times get them removed.

Credit Inquiries

This section contains the names of those who obtained a copy of your credit report. Inquiries remain on your report up to two years.

	EXPERIAN	EQUIFAX	TRANSUNION
POPLAR BLUFF Finance other than personal 2/25/2010			✓
POPLAR BLUFF Finance other than personal 1/22/2010			✓
HSBC RETAIL SERVICES All Banks 12/20/2009		✓	

STAN MORRIS

1ST PER Banks and S&Ls 11/21/2009			✓
CREDS Miscellaneous and public record 10/28/2009			✓
CA Credit card and travel / entertainment companies 10/23/2009			✓
ATMOB Telephone Companies 9/21/2009		✓	
CAL ONE Auto Financing 6/12/2009		✓	
COF Finance, personal 6/12/2009			✓
CIAL AUTO Auto Financing 5/29/2009	✓	✓	
C ONE Auto Financing 5/29/2009		✓	
CF Finance, personal 5/29/2009			✓
ROANS Auto Financing 5/25/2009		✓	
CONE Auto Financing 5/15/2009	✓	✓	
CAF Finance, personal 5/15/2009			✓
CASE Banks and S&Ls 5/15/2009			✓
CRED Miscellaneous and public record 5/15/2009			✓
CRED Miscellaneous and public record 5/14/2009			✓
DTV Miscellaneous Utilities 4/12/2009		✓	
GAC Credit card and			✓

THE COMPLETE CREDIT CARE™ PROGRAM

travel / entertainment companies 4/6/2009			
CASE Banks and S&Ls 4/6/2009			✓
CONE Auto Financing 4/4/2009	✓	✓	
C Finance, personal 4/4/2009			✓
CRED Miscellaneous and public record 4/4/2009			✓
CF Finance, personal 4/4/2009			✓
CRED Auto Reseller 3/21/2009	✓		✓
PFF Finance other than personal 3/20/2009			✓
SCRDT Miscellaneous and public record 2/20/2009			✓
MOOLS Miscellaneous 12/10/2008		✓	
PFF Finance other than personal 11/28/2008			✓
CL AUTO Auto Financing 10/27/2008	✓	✓	
CONE Auto Financing 10/27/2008		✓	
WANK Automotive 10/27/2008			✓
CASE Banks and S&Ls 10/27/2008			✓
CF Finance, personal 10/27/2008			✓
CRED Miscellaneous and public record 10/27/2008			✓
AINCL Collection services 9/26/2008			✓

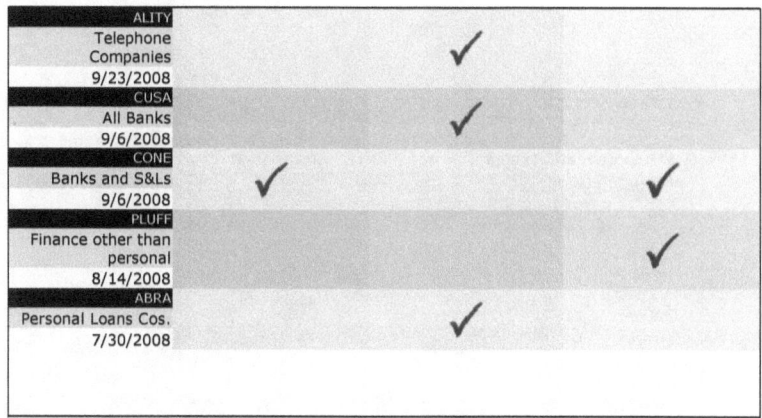

Credit Inquiries can hurt your overall score. There was supposed to be a change in this with the new FICO scoring model in 2010 but I haven't seen it yet. If you have too many inquires on your bureau then it is possible to hurt your score. I've seen as many as 60 on one report over a 2 week period. This report was hurt badly. These stay on your report for at least 24 months.

THE COMPLETE CREDIT CARE ™ PROGRAM

Account History

This section contains specific information on each account you've opened in the past. Positive information about your accounts remains on your report indefinitely.

NFIN

	EXPERIAN	EQUIFAX	TRANSUNION
Account Name:	NFN/55		NFN/55
Account Number:	48xxXXXX	48xxXXXX	48xxXXXX
Acct Type:	Collection Department / Agency / Attorney	Collection Account	Collection Account
Acct Status:	Closed		Open
Monthly Payment:			
Date Open:	8/1/2009	8/1/2009	8/7/2009
Balance:	$208.00	$208.00	$208.00
Terms:	1 Month		
High Balance:			
Limit:			
Past Due:	$208.00		
Payment Status:	Seriously past due date / assigned to attorney, collection agency, or credit grantor's internal collection department	Unpaid	Collection account
Comments:		MEDICAL Unpaid	Placed for collection

24-Month Payment History   ? Legend

Date:	Oct	Nov	Dec	Jan	Feb	Mar	Apr	May	Jun	Jul	Aug	Sep	Oct	Nov	Dec	Jan	Feb	Mar	Apr	May	Jun	Jul	Aug	Sep
Experian:																								
Equifax:	07	07	07	08	08	08	08	08	08	08	08	08	08	08	09	09	09	09	09	09	09	09	09	09
TransUnion:																								KD

This account has some problems. To begin with it doesn't belong to this person. In this case this man had an ex that used my clients social security number when they went to the hospital. The first thing we did was call Equifax and place a fraud alert on this client's account. Then we disputed the account and ask for documents that backed up the allegation of collection. The bureaus responded back in 45 days and claimed they had verified the account to be my clients and didn't take it off. My client disputed the account again and insisted they prove it to be his. They couldn't prove it and took it off. Letters were sent to all three bureaus.

Another problem with this account, which could be disputed, is that the record is incomplete. Look at the open lines. TransUnion shows it open. Experian shows it closed. There are no amounts or terms or past due figures on some of the bureaus. This is incomplete data. Remember FCRA maintains that accounts have to be accurate. An account cannot be accurate with incomplete data. This is a reason to dispute, other than fraud, if necessary.

	EXPERIAN	EQUIFAX	TRANSUNION
Account Name:			
Account Number:		10XXXX	
Acct Type:		Collection Account	
Acct Status:			
Monthly Payment:			
Date Open:		1/1/2008	
Balance:		$63.00	
Terms:			
High Balance:			
Limit:			
Past Due:			
Payment Status:		Unpaid	
Comments:		MEDICAL Unpaid	

24-Month Payment History ? Legend

Date:	Jan	Feb	Mar	Apr	May	Jun	Jul	Aug	Sep	Oct	Nov	Dec	Jan	Feb	Mar	Apr	May	Jun	Jul	Aug	Sep	Oct	Nov	Dec
Experian:	-	-	-	-	-	-	-	-	-	-	-	-	-	-	-	-	-	-	-	-	-	-	-	-
Equifax:																								
TransUnion:																								

Above is a good example of CRA's blunders that cost you precious credit score points.

Here is another account where the data is incomplete. Notice there is no one claiming to collect this account. Here is a good one that needs to be disputed.

THE COMPLETE CREDIT CARE ™ PROGRAM

NoMEDCLR

	EXPERIAN	EQUIFAX	TRANSUNION
Account Name:	NOMEDCLR		NOMEDCLR
Account Number:	53x36XXXX	53x36XXXX	53x36XXXX
Acct Type:	Unknown - Credit Extension, Review, Or Collection	Open Account	Collection Account
Acct Status:	Closed		Open
Monthly Payment:			
Date Open:	10/1/2009	10/1/2009	10/14/2009
Balance:	$262.00	$262.00	$262.00
Terms:	1 Month		
High Balance:		$262.00	
Limit:			
Past Due:	$262.00	$262.00	
Payment Status:	Seriously past due date / assigned to attorney, collection agency, or credit grantor's internal collection department	At least 120 days or more than four payments past due	Collection account
Comments:		MEDICAL COLLECTION ACCOUNT	Placed for collection

24-Month Payment History ? Legend

Date:	Nov	Dec	Jan	Feb	Mar	Apr	May	Jun	Jul	Aug	Sep	Oct	Nov	Dec	Jan	Feb	Mar	Apr	May	Jun	Jul	Aug	Sep	Oct
Experian:																								
Equifax:	07	07	08	08	08	08	08	08	08	08	08	08	08	08	09	09	09	09	09	09	09	09	09	09
TransUnion:																								OK

Here is a collection account that is starting to show positive once again on one of the bureaus. Notice that TransUnion and Equifax are still showing it open. We need to dispute the account as closed. Have them go back to the Experian close date and report it closed. Another way to dispute this is to ask for a delete. Ask TransUnion and Equifax to delete it on the grounds that it is reporting open and it is in fact closed and it is hurting your score. Ask Experian to delete it because the information is incomplete. When was it closed?

When sending the dispute to TransUnion, mark out the Equifax entry.
When sending the dispute to Equifax mark out the TransUnion item.
Circle the Experian as proof, on each dispute letter, that the others are reporting the item wrong.

When disputing the Experian mark out the other two and just state this item is incomplete. It has no close date; Ask them to delete the item.

Notice the green OK under Oct 09. If you can't get Experian to delete this one it won't be the end of the world. It's starting to go green on the history segment under the items.

STAN MORRIS

NOMEDCLR

	EXPERIAN	EQUIFAX	TRANSUNION
Account Name:	NOMEDCLR		NO MEDCLR
Account Number:	4892XXXX	4892XXXX	4892XXXX
Acct Type:	Unknown - Credit Extension, Review, Or Collection	Open Account	Collection Account
Acct Status:	Closed		Open
Monthly Payment:			
Date Open:	1/1/2009	1/1/2009	1/16/2009
Balance:	$195.00	$137.00	$133.00
Terms:	1 Month		
High Balance:		$137.00	
Limit:			
Past Due:	$195.00	$137.00	
Payment Status:	Seriously past due date / assigned to attorney, collection agency, or credit grantor's internal collection department	At least 120 days or more than four payments past due	Collection account
Comments:		MEDICAL COLLECTION ACCOUNT	Placed for collection

24-Month Payment History ? Legend

Date:	May	Jun	Jul	Aug	Sep	Oct	Nov	Dec	Jan	Feb	Mar	Apr	May	Jun	Jul	Aug	Sep	Oct	Nov	Dec	Jan	Feb	Mar	Apr
Experian:																								
Equifax:	07	07	07	07	07	07	07	07	08	08	08	08	08	08	08	08	08	08	08	08	09	09	09	09
TransUnion:																					OK	OK	OK	KD OK

Here is another collection account that will begin to hurt your score less. In fact this is a good example why you should monitor your credit report every month during your credit repair efforts. This account has a problem with TransUnion and Equifax. Experian is showing it closed. Dispute this account to the two bureaus that have it open. Show the other two bureaus that it is closed and that the way they are reporting this account as OPEN is hurting your credit score. Ask them to report the account like they are reporting the Experian item. Make a copy of the item and prove to them that Experian is reporting it CLOSED. Black out the Equifax item on the letter you send Transunion and black out the Transunion item on the letter you send Equifax.

THE COMPLETE CREDIT CARE ™ PROGRAM

NOMEDCLR			
	EXPERIAN	**EQUIFAX**	**TRANSUNION**
Account Name:	NOMEDCLR		NOMEDCLR
Account Number:	4892XXXX	4892XXXX	4892XXXX
Acct Type:	Unknown - Credit Extension, Review, Or Collection	Open Account	Collection Account
Acct Status:	Closed		Open
Monthly Payment:			
Date Open:	1/1/2009	1/1/2009	1/16/2009
Balance:	$382.00	$379.00	$372.00
Terms:	1 Month		
High Balance:		$372.00	
Limit:			
Past Due:	$372.00	$372.00	
Payment Status:	Seriously past due date / assigned to attorney, collection agency, or credit grantor's internal collection department	At least 120 days or more than four payments past due	Collection account
Comments:		MEDICAL COLLECTION ACCOUNT	Placed for collection

24-Month Payment History ? Legend

Date:	May	Jun	Jul	Aug	Sep	Oct	Nov	Dec	Jan	Feb	Mar	Apr	May	Jun	Jul	Aug	Sep	Oct	Nov	Dec	Jan	Feb	Mar	Apr
Experian: Equifax:	07	07	07	07	07	07	07	07	08	08	08	08	08	08	08	08	08	08	08	08	09	09	09	09
TransUnion:																								KD
																				OK	OK	OK	OK	OK

Notice that the past few accounts have errors. Look at the accounts and see if all the accounts have the same amount for collection. This is another way to dispute what the bureaus report. There is no way that this collection item can be accurate.

STAN MORRIS

NOMEDCLR			
	EXPERIAN	**EQUIFAX**	**TRANSUNION**
Account Name:	NOMEDCLR		NOMEDCLR
Account Number:	4892XXXX	4892XXXX	4892XXXX
Acct Type:	Unknown - Credit Extension, Review, Or Collection	Open Account	Collection Account
Acct Status:	Closed		Open
Monthly Payment:			
Date Open:	1/1/2009	2/1/2009	1/16/2009
Balance:	$119.00	$133.00	$137.00
Terms:	1 Month		
High Balance:		$133.00	
Limit:	$0	$0	$0
Past Due:	$133.00	$133.00	
Payment Status:	Seriously past due date / assigned to attorney, collection agency, or credit grantor's internal collection department	At least 120 days or more than four payments past due	Collection account
Comments:		MEDICAL COLLECTION ACCOUNT	Placed for collection

24-Month Payment History ? Legend

Date:	May	Jun	Jul	Aug	Sep	Oct	Nov	Dec	Jan	Feb	Mar	Apr	May	Jun	Jul	Aug	Sep	Oct	Nov	Dec	Jan	Feb	Mar	Apr
Experian:																								
Equifax:	07	07	0/7	07	07	07	07	07	08	08	08	08	08	08	0/8	08	08	08	08	08	09	09	09	09
TransUnion:																								KD
																					OK	OK	OK	OK

Can you pick up on all the things wrong on this account? Credit limits lower than high balance. Different amounts are owed at each bureau. There are different dates. Some are showing open and Some showing closed. Remember FCRA says the information must be accurate. Which account is accurate? Are any of them accurate? I would start off disputing this one by showing the information reported as inaccurate. The balance showing owed is higher than the limit. Also note the red KD in 09. This account is hurting the credit score and must be fixed.

THE COMPLETE CREDIT CARE™ PROGRAM

NOMEDCLR

	EXPERIAN	EQUIFAX	TRANSUNION
Account Name:	NOMEDCLR		NOMEDCLR
Account Number:	4892XXXX	4892XXXX	4892XXXX
Acct Type:	Unknown - Credit Extension, Review, Or Collection	Open Account	Collection Account
Acct Status:	Closed		Open
Monthly Payment:			
Date Open:	1/1/2009	1/1/2009	1/16/2009
Balance:	$137.00	$195.00	$195.00
Terms:	1 Month		
High Balance:		$195.00	
Limit:			
Past Due:	$137.00	$195.00	
Payment Status:	Seriously past due date / assigned to attorney, collection agency, or credit grantor's internal collection department	At least 120 days or more than four payments past due	Collection account
Comments:		MEDICAL COLLECTION ACCOUNT	Placed for collection

24-Month Payment History ? Legend

Date:	May	Jun	Jul	Aug	Sep	Oct	Nov	Dec	Jan	Feb	Mar	Apr	May	Jun	Jul	Aug	Sep	Oct	Nov	Dec	Jan	Feb	Mar	Apr
Experian Equifax:	07	07	07	07	07	07	07	07	08	08	08	08	08	08	08	08	08	08	08	08	09	09	09	09
TransUnion:																				KD	OK	OK	OK	OK

Here's an account which must be dealt with now. It has Open and Closed designations with different bureaus. The most damaging part is the red KD. This is a major key derogatory item. I would initially dispute this item as being inaccurate. How can the information be accurate at Experian, accurate in TransUnion and Equifax as well? Dispute the TransUnion account as inaccurate and send them a copy of this item proving they are reporting it wrong. Mark out the Equifax before you send it. Ask Trans union to delete this item. Do the same thing with Equifax and mark out the TransUnion item.

STAN MORRIS

AARAGNCY

	EXPERIAN	EQUIFAX	TRANSUNION
Account Name:	AARAGENCY INC		AARAGNCY
Account Number:	3XX		3XX
Acct Type:	Collection Department / Agency / Attorney		Collection Account
Acct Status:	Closed		Open
Monthly Payment:			
Date Open:	10/1/2008		10/25/2008
Balance:	$156.00		$156.00
Terms:	Unknown		
High Balance:			
Limit:			
Past Due:	$156.00		
Payment Status:	Seriously past due date / assigned to attorney, collection agency, or credit grantor's internal collection department		Collection account
Comments:			Placed for collection

24-Month Payment History ? Legend

Date:	Apr	May	Jun	Jul	Aug	Sep	Oct	Nov	Dec	Jan	Feb	Mar	Apr	May	Jun	Jul	Aug	Sep	Oct	Nov	Dec	Jan	Feb	Mar
Experian: Equifax:	07	07	07	07	07	07	07	07	07	08	08	08	08	08	08	08	08	08	08	08	08	09	09	09
TransUnion:	ND	ND	ND	ND	ND	ND	ND	ND	ND	ND	ND	ND	ND	ND	ND	ND	ND	ND	ND	ND	KD	ND	ND	KD

The above account is reporting incorrectly on one of the bureaus. I would dispute them both. I have had success disputing the fact I've never done business with this company. If I had a car and I came to your house and you answered the door and I shoved a title to the car in your face and said pay me, what would you do? You'd think I was crazy because you had never agreed to buy that car. I can't force you to pay me because I can't force you to do business with me. That is exactly what collection agencies are doing. They are trying to force you to do business with them. You've never signed any document of any kind for any goods and services from the collection agency. So thereby you've never agreed to do business with them. I'm not a lawyer but I'm not sure you are obligated to pay them. There will be more on collection agencies and how to deal with them later.

THE COMPLETE CREDIT CARE ™ PROGRAM

FSTPR

	EXPERIAN	EQUIFAX	TRANSUNION
Account Name:	FIRST PNK	FIER	FSTIER
Account Number:	58XXXX	58XXXX	58XXXX
Acct Type:	Credit Card - Revolving Terms	Revolving or Option	Revolving account
Acct Status:	Open		Open
Monthly Payment:	$7.00	$7.00	$7.00
Date Open:	12/1/2009	12/1/2009	12/3/2009
Balance:	$7.00	$7.00	$7.00
Terms:	Revolving		Minimum
High Balance:	$247.00		$247.00
Limit:	$250.00	$250.00	$250.00
Past Due:			$0.00
Payment Status:	Current	Pays account as agreed	Paid or paying as agreed
Comments:		CREDIT CARD	

24-Month Payment History   ? Legend

Date:	Mar	Apr	May	Jun	Jul	Aug	Sep	Oct	Nov	Dec	Jan	Feb	Mar	Apr	May	Jun	Jul	Aug	Sep	Oct	Nov	Dec	Jan	Feb
Experian:																								
Equifax:	08	08	08	08	08	08	08	08	08	08	09	09	09	09	09	09	09	09	09	09	09	09	10	10
TransUnion:																				OK	OK	OK	OK	OK
																				OK	OK	OK	OK	OK
																				OK	OK	OK	OK	OK

Finally a good account

STAN MORRIS

FSTIER

	EXPERIAN	EQUIFAX	TRANSUNION
Account Name:	FER BANK	FEMIER	FMIER
Account Number:	5XXXX	5XXXX	5XXXX
Acct Type:	Credit Card - Revolving Terms	Revolving or Option	Revolving account
Acct Status:	Closed		Closed
Monthly Payment:			
Date Open:	12/1/2005	12/1/2005	12/15/2005
Balance:		$0.00	$0.00
Terms:	Revolving		
High Balance:		$414.00	$414.00
Limit:	$250.00		$300.00
Past Due:			$0.00
Payment Status:	Charge-off	Bad debt & placed for collection & skip	Charged off as bad debt
Comments:		CHARGED OFF ACCOUNT CREDIT CARD	Profit and loss writeoff

24-Month Payment History   ? Legend

Date:	Oct	Nov	Dec	Jan	Feb	Mar	Apr	May	Jun	Jul	Aug	Sep	Oct	Nov	Dec	Jan	Feb	Mar	Apr	May	Jun	Jul	Aug	Sep
Experian:																								
Equifax:	06	06	06	07	07	07	07	07	07	07	07	07	07	07	07	08	08	08	08	08	08	08	08	08
TransUnion:	KD	KD	KD	KD	KD	KD	KD	KD OK	KD	KD	KD	KD	KD	KD	KD	KD	KD	KD	KD	KD	KD OK	KD	KD
	OK	OK	OK	OK	OK	OK	OK		OK	OK	OK	OK	OK	OK	OK	OK	OK	OK	OK	OK		OK	OK

Don't worry about this one right now because it is not hurting the score because of its age as much as one that is under two years old. It will turn green in the history in Sept. 2010 as long as it's closed in 2008. Once you have the more recent ones improved then look at the ones that show Key Derogatory. If after you investigate the age and how it's reporting make sure it won't hurt your score if it's removed. Here's a tip. It may be an old account that's giving you 5 years of history. If it's not hurting your account it may be helping because of its age.

THE COMPLETE CREDIT CARE ™ PROGRAM

FRANCOL

	EXPERIAN	EQUIFAX	TRANSUNION
Account Name:	FRANLLECTION SV	FRANCTION	FRANKCOL
Account Number:	19XXXX	19XXXX	19XXXX
Acct Type:	Collection Department / Agency / Attorney	Collection Account	Collection Account
Acct Status:	Closed		Open
Monthly Payment:			
Date Open:	7/1/2008	7/1/2008	7/19/2008
Balance:	$143.00	$143.00	$143.00
Terms:	1 Month		
High Balance:			
Limit:			
Past Due:	$143.00		
Payment Status:	Seriously past due date / assigned to attorney, collection agency, or credit grantor's internal collection department	Unpaid	Collection account
Comments:		Unpaid	Placed for collection

24-Month Payment History ? Legend

Date:	Sep	Oct	Nov	Dec	Jan	Feb	Mar	Apr	May	Jun	Jul	Aug	Sep	Oct	Nov	Dec	Jan	Feb	Mar	Apr	May	Jun	Jul	Aug
Experian:																								
Equifax:	06	06	06	06	07	07	07	07	07	07	07	07	07	07	07	07	08	08	08	08	08	08	08	08
TransUnion:																								KD

Another 'I've never done business with this company before' letter.

STAN MORRIS

G C SERVICES

	EXPERIAN	EQUIFAX	TRANSUNION
Account Name:	G C SERVICES	G C SERVICES	
Account Number:	837XXXX	87XXXX	
Acct Type:	Collection Department / Agency / Attorney	Collection Account	
Acct Status:	Closed		
Monthly Payment:			
Date Open:	2/1/2010	2/1/2010	
Balance:		$99.00	
Terms:	1 Month		
High Balance:			
Limit:			
Past Due:			
Payment Status:	Paid, was a collection account, insurance claim or government claim or was terminated for default	Unpaid	
Comments:		Unpaid	

24-Month Payment History   ? Legend

Date:	May	Jun	Jul	Aug	Sep	Oct	Nov	Dec	Jan	Feb	Mar	Apr	May	Jun	Jul	Aug	Sep	Oct	Nov	Dec	Jan	Feb	Mar	Apr
Experian:																								
Equifax:	06	06	06	06	06	06	06	06	07	07	07	07	07	07	07	07	07	07	07	07	08	08	08	08
TransUnion:																							KD	OK

Here's one just turning OK with Experian but not showing closed with Equifax. I'd dispute it with Equifax and ask for a deletion because of incorrect information.

THE COMPLETE CREDIT CARE ™ PROGRAM

GC SERVICES	EXPERIAN	EQUIFAX	TRANSUNION
Account Name:		G C SS	GC SS
Account Number:		87XXXX	87XXXX
Acct Type:		Collection Account	Collection Account
Acct Status:			Closed
Monthly Payment:			
Date Open:		1/1/2008	1/3/2008
Balance:		$0.00	$0.00
Terms:			
High Balance:			
Limit:			
Past Due:			
Payment Status:		Paid	Payment after charge off / collection
Comments:		Paid	Paid collection

24-Month Payment History ? Legend

Date:	Jan	Feb	Mar	Apr	May	Jun	Jul	Aug	Sep	Oct	Nov	Dec	Jan	Feb	Mar	Apr	May	Jun	Jul	Aug	Sep	Oct	Nov	Dec
Experian:	-	-	-	-	-	-	-	-	-	-	-	-	-	-	-	-	-	-	-	-	-	-	-	-
Equifax:																								
TransUnion:																								

Paid collections are very hard to get removed. However if you see incomplete or unverifiable or incorrect information it would be worth looking into.

STAN MORRIS

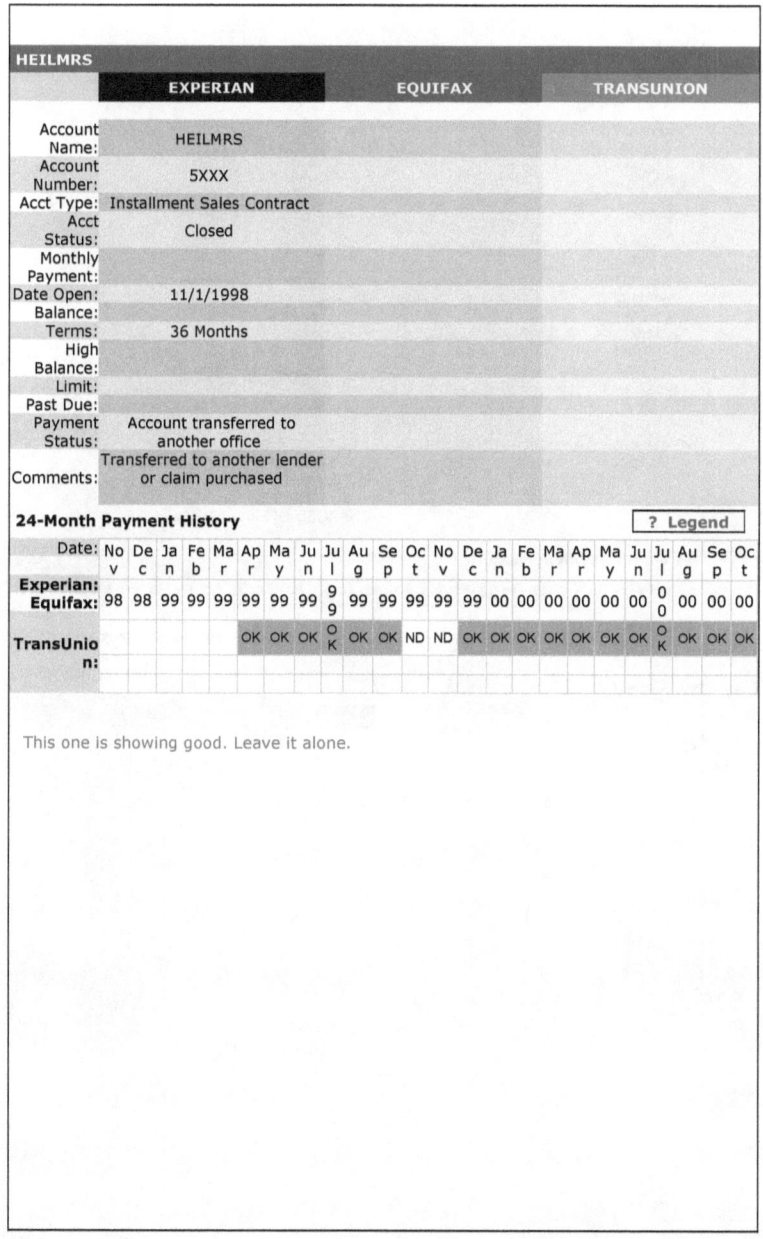

This one is showing good. Leave it alone.

THE COMPLETE CREDIT CARE ™ PROGRAM

HS BANK

	EXPERIAN	EQUIFAX	TRANSUNION
Account Name:	HS BANK	HS BANK	
Account Number:	54XXXX	44XXXX	
Acct Type:	Credit Card - Revolving Terms	Revolving or Option	
Acct Status:	Closed		
Monthly Payment:			
Date Open:	12/1/2005	12/1/2005	
Balance:		$0.00	
Terms:	Revolving		
High Balance:		$189.00	
Limit:	$0.00		
Past Due:			
Payment Status:	Account transferred to another office	Bad debt & placed for collection & skip	
Comments:	Transferred to another lender or claim purchased	ACCOUNT TRANSFERRED OR SOLD CHARGED OFF ACCOUNT	

24-Month Payment History ? Legend

Date:	Sept	Oct	Nov	Dec	Jan	Feb	Mar	Apr	May	Jun	Jul	Aug	Sep	Oct	Nov	Dec	Jan	Feb	Mar	Apr	May	Jun	Jul	Aug
Experian: Equifax:	05	05	05	05	06	06	06	06	06	06	06	06	06	06	06	06	07	07	07	07	07	07	07	07
					OK	OK	OK	OK	OK	30	60	90	120	120	KD	KD	ND	ND	ND	ND	ND	ND	ND	OK
TransUnion:					OK	OK	OK	OK	OK	OK	30	60	90	120	120	OK	OK	OK	OK	OK	OK	NDOK	NDOK	OK

This one we'll clean up later. It's showing green and isn't hurting the score as badly as others. It is a good example of one that you might see that has incorrect aging. See the yellow square that is showing 120 days in October and Nov of 2006. This is an error that you can dispute with an account that is younger than two years old. This is called aging and is not right.

STAN MORRIS

HS BANK			
	EXPERIAN	**EQUIFAX**	**TRANSUNION**
Account Name:			HS BANK
Account Number:			5XXXX
Acct Type:			Revolving account
Acct Status:			Closed
Monthly Payment:			
Date Open:			12/13/2005
Balance:			$0.00
Terms:			
High Balance:			$452.00
Limit:			$0.00
Past Due:			$0.00
Payment Status:			Charged off as bad debt
Comments:			Purchased by another lender

24-Month Payment History ? Legend

Date:	Jan	Feb	Mar	Apr	May	Jun	Jul	Aug	Sep	Oct	Nov	Dec	Jan	Feb	Mar	Apr	May	Jun	Jul	Aug	Sep	Oct	Nov	Dec
Experian:	-	-	-	-	-	-	-	-	-	-	-	-	-	-	-	-	-	-	-	-	-	-	-	-
Equifax:																								
TransUnion:																								

Remember a charged-off debt that is closed will never help your score. This item is over two years old. It isn't hurting your score as badly as a younger charge-off would. It is one to investigate after you get the more pressing problems corrected.

THE COMPLETE CREDIT CARE ™ PROGRAM

MERCCEPT	EXPERIAN	EQUIFAX	TRANSUNION
Account Name:	MERCEPTANCE	MERPTANCE	MERCCEPT
Account Number:	A81XXXX	A81XXXX	A81XXXX
Acct Type:	Installment Sales Contract	Installment	Installment account
Acct Status:	Closed		Closed
Monthly Payment:		$59.00	$59.00
Date Open:	3/1/2007	3/1/2007	3/28/2007
Balance:		$0.00	$0.00
Terms:	36 Months		36 X
High Balance:		$2,126.00	$2,126.00
Limit:			
Past Due:			$0.00
Payment Status:	Paid, was a charge-off	Pays account as agreed	Charged off as bad debt
Comments:		PAID ACCOUNT / ZERO BALANCE	Closed

24-Month Payment History   ? Legend

Date:	Mar	Apr	May	Jun	Jul	Aug	Sep	Oct	Nov	Dec	Jan	Feb	Mar	Apr	May	Jun	Jul	Aug	Sep	Oct	Nov	Dec	Jan	Feb
Experian: Equifax:	07	07	07	07	07	07	07	07	07	07	08	08	08	08	08	08	08	08	08	08	08	08	09	09
TransUnion:						KD	KD	KD	KD	KD	KD	KD	KD	KD	KD	KD	KD	KD	KD	KD	KD	KD	KD	OK
	OK	KD	OK	OK	OK	OK	OK	OK	OK	OK	OK	OK	OK	OK	OK	OK	OK	OK	OK	OK	OK	OK	OK	OK

See the green in 2009. This one is reporting positive again. Leave it alone.

STAN MORRIS

MERACCEPTANCE

	EXPERIAN	EQUIFAX	TRANSUNION
Account Name:	MERCCEPTANCE	MERCCEPTANCE	
Account Number:	A01XXXX	A01XXXX	
Acct Type:	Installment Sales Contract	Installment	
Acct Status:	Open		
Monthly Payment:	$59.00	$59.00	
Date Open:	3/1/2007	3/1/2007	
Balance:	$2,126.00	$2,126.00	
Terms:	36 Months		
High Balance:		$2,126.00	
Limit:			
Past Due:	$59.00	$177.00	
Payment Status:	Past due 30 days	not more than four payments past due	
Comments:			

24-Month Payment History   ? Legend

Date:	Aug	Sep	Oct	Nov	Dec	Jan	Feb	Mar	Apr	May	Jun	Jul	Aug	Sep	Oct	Nov	Dec	Jan	Feb	Mar	Apr	May	Jun	Jul
Experian Equifax:	05	05	05	05	05	06	06	06	06	06	06	06	06	06	06	06	06	07	07	07	07	07	07	07
TransUnion:																					OK	OK	OK	OK
																					30	30	60	

This one can be worked on after we fix the younger items. The yellow is three years ago. When you do dispute the item you could initially dispute them both as inaccurate data because the amounts are different in the past due column. Secondly, Experian doesn't show a high balance and Equifax doesn't report any terms. This second dispute would be asking for a delete because of incomplete data on both bureaus.

THE COMPLETE CREDIT CARE ™ PROGRAM

MIDCRED	EXPERIAN	EQUIFAX	TRANSUNION
Account Name:	MIGMT	MAG	MRED
Account Number:	852178XXXX	852178XXXX	852178XXXX
Acct Type:	Unknown - Credit Extension, Review, Or Collection	Open Account	Collection Account
Acct Status:	Closed		Open
Monthly Payment:			
Date Open:	2/1/2007	2/1/2007	2/9/2007
Balance:	$1,223.00	$1,223.00	$1,223.00
Terms:	1 Month		
High Balance:		$821.00	
Limit:			
Past Due:	$1,223.00	$1,223.00	
Payment Status:	Seriously past due date / assigned to attorney, collection agency, or credit grantor's internal collection department	At least 120 days or more than four payments past due	Collection account
Comments:		COLLECTION ACCOUNT	Placed for collection

24-Month Payment History   ? Legend

Date:	Mar	Apr	May	Jun	Jul	Aug	Sep	Oct	Nov	Dec	Jan	Feb	Mar	Apr	May	Jun	Jul	Aug	Sep	Oct	Nov	Dec	Jan	Feb
Experian:																								
Equifax:	08	08	08	08	08	08	08	08	08	08	09	09	09	09	09	09	09	09	09	09	09	09	10	10
TransUnion:	ND	ND	ND	ND	ND	KD	KD	KD	KD	KD	KD	KD	KD	KD	KD	KD	KD	KD	ND	ND	ND	ND	KD
	OK	OK	OK	OK	OK	OK	OK	OK	OK	OK	OK	OK	OK	OK	OK	OK	OK	OK	OK	OK	OK	OK	OK	OK

Any time you see a RED KD figure out how you can ethically dispute the item. If you show a key derogatory within the last two years, get it off your credit report. It's killing your score. I would dispute this one as incomplete. I would simply say the information is incomplete and let them figure out what isn't there. I'd also look at disputing the account being closed at Experian and the others showing it open.

NFIN	EXPERIAN	EQUIFAX	TRANSUNION
Account Name:		NC	
Account Number:		1969XXXX	
Acct Type:		Open Account	
Acct Status:			
Monthly Payment:			
Date Open:		1/1/0001	
Balance:		$295.00	
Terms:			
High Balance:		$295.00	
Limit:			
Past Due:		$295.00	
Payment Status:		At least 120 days or more than four payments past due	
Comments:		COLLECTION ACCOUNT	

24-Month Payment History ? Legend

Date:	Apr	May	Jun	Jul	Aug	Sep	Oct	Nov	Dec	Jan	Feb	Mar
Experian:												
Equifax:	06	06	06	06	06	06	06	06	06	07	07	07
TransUnion:	OK	OK	OK	OK	OK	OK	OK	OK	OK	OK	OK	OK

Date:	Apr	May	Jun	Jul	Aug	Sep	Oct	Nov	Dec	Jan	Feb	Mar
Experian:												
Equifax:	07	07	07	07	07	07	07	07	07	08	08	08
TransUnion:	OK	OK	OK	OK	OK	OK	OK	OK	OK	OK	OK	OK

Here's one that shows open. The statute of limitations is up on this one. I'd ask for it to be shown as closed. You might leave it alone and make it one of the last things you dispute. It's reporting in a way that's probably not hurting your score right now. Keep in mind any time you dispute a collection the credit bureau will give updated information to the collection agency. They may decide to start trying to collect the account once again. The only way I think anyone could collect on this account is if there has been payment activity within the statute of limitations, period. I'm not a lawyer. That's my opinion.

THE COMPLETE CREDIT CARE ™ PROGRAM

PLF CU

	EXPERIAN	EQUIFAX	TRANSUNION
Account Name:		PLUFF FEDERAL	PLF CU
Account Number:		1XXXX	1XXXX
Acct Type:		Open Account	Installment account
Acct Status:			Closed
Monthly Payment:			$298.00
Date Open:		11/1/2003	11/14/2003
Balance:			$0.00
Terms:		101 s	28 Months
High Balance:		$2,081.00	$7,746.00
Limit:			
Past Due:			$0.00
Payment Status:		Pays account as agreed	Paid or paying as agreed
Comments:		LINE OF CREDIT	Closed

24-Month Payment History   ? Legend

Date:	Mar	Apr	May	Jun	Jul	Aug	Sep	Oct	Nov	Dec	Jan	Feb	Mar	Apr	May	Jun	Jul	Aug	Sep	Oct	Nov	Dec	Jan	Feb
Experian:																								
Equifax:	03	03	03	03	03	03	03	03	03	03	04	04	04	04	04	04	04	04	04	04	04	04	05	05
TransUnion:								OK	OK	OK	OK	OK	OK	OK	OK	OK	OK	OK	OK	OK	OK	OK	OK	OK
							OK	OK	ND															

This one might help if Equifax showed closed as well. It might bring down the debt to income ratio that lenders use to make sure you're not borrowing too much money. I would ask Equifax to report it closed. NOTE******Do not ask them to delete this account. Ask them to report it as closed.

STAN MORRIS

PRLF CU	EXPERIAN	EQUIFAX	TRANSUNION
Account Name:		PUFF FEDERAL	PLF CU
Account Number:		12xxx	12xxx
Acct Type:		Open Account	Installment account
Acct Status:			Open
Monthly Payment:			$401.00
Date Open:		1/1/2004	1/28/2004
Balance:			$9,929.00
Terms:		598 s	60 Months
High Balance:		$24,418.00	$24,418.00
Limit:			
Past Due:			$0.00
Payment Status:		Pays account as agreed	Paid or paying as agreed
Comments:		AUTO	

24-Month Payment History

Date:	Feb	Mar	Apr	May	Jun	Jul	Aug	Sep	Oct	Nov	Dec	Jan	Feb	Mar	Apr	May	Jun	Jul	Aug	Sep	Oct	Nov	Dec	Jan
Experian:																								
Equifax:	08	08	08	08	08	08	08	08	08	08	09	09	09	09	09	09	09	09	09	09	09	09	09	10
TransUnion:	OK	OK	OK	OK	OK	OK	OK	OK	OK	OK	OK	OK	OK	OK	OK	OK	OK	OK	OK	OK	OK	OK	OK	OK

Here is a good account. It's been established since 2004 It shows the client pays well. It has a good balance. It has a great credit high amount. See the 598 s on Equifax. Leave it alone. The only thing you might want to do is to get Experian to report it, as well. Simply make a copy of this page and show Experian that the others are reporting it and ask them to report it, as well.

THE COMPLETE CREDIT CARE ™ PROGRAM

PLF CU

	EXPERIAN	EQUIFAX	TRANSUNION
Account Name:		PLUFF FEDERAL	PLF CU
Account Number:		4xxx	4xxxx
Acct Type:		Open Account	Installment account
Acct Status:			Closed
Monthly Payment:			$315.00
Date Open:		3/1/2000	3/24/2000
Balance:		$0.00	$0.00
Terms:		315 s	60 Months
High Balance:		$20,983.00	$20,983.00
Limit:			
Past Due:			$0.00
Payment Status:		Pays account as agreed	Paid or paying as agreed
Comments:		PAID ACCOUNT / ZERO BALANCE AUTO	

24-Month Payment History   **? Legend**

Date:	Aug	Sep	Oct	Nov	Dec	Jan	Feb	Mar	Apr	May	Jun	Jul	Aug	Sep	Oct	Nov	Dec	Jan	Feb	Mar	Apr	May	Jun	Jul
Experian:																								
Equifax:	02	02	02	02	02	03	03	03	03	03	03	03	03	03	03	03	03	04	04	04	04	04	04	04
TransUnion:		OK	OK	OK	OK	OK	OK	OK	OK	OK	30	OK	30	60	60	OK	OK	OK	OK	OK	OK			OK
	OK	OK	OK	ND	OK	OK	OK	OK	OK	ND	30	ND	30	OK	60	60	OK	ND	OK	OK	ND	OK		OK

We won't dispute this one but here are a couple of reasons to dispute when you see ones under two years old.

If this one had been one we needed to dispute we would have disputed on the grounds that the information was inaccurate. We would have asked them to verify and delete this account. Look at the dates. We would not point to the dates. We would make them find which ones weren't correct.

Also note there are 2 months that show 60 days past due in a row. Only dispute one thing at a time when writing dispute letters. You might need the other reason for a second dispute later. This is a common error caused by aging an account. There is no way you can be 60 days past due two months in a row. There's no way to be 30, 60, 90, or 120 days late more than once in a row. Re-aging accounts is illegal. Credit card companies are notorious for doing this. If you see this, dispute it.

STAN MORRIS

P B FEDERAL			
	EXPERIAN	**EQUIFAX**	**TRANSUNION**
Account Name:		P B FEDERAL	
Account Number:		116XXXX	
Acct Type:		Open Account	
Acct Status:			
Monthly Payment:			
Date Open:		11/1/2003	
Balance:		$0.00	
Terms:		298 s	
High Balance:		$7,746.00	
Limit:			
Past Due:			
Payment Status:		Pays account as agreed	
Comments:		PAID ACCOUNT / ZERO BALANCE AUTO	

24-Month Payment History   ? Legend

Date:	Mar	Apr	May	Jun	Jul	Aug	Sep	Oct	Nov	Dec	Jan	Feb	Mar	Apr	May	Jun	Jul	Aug	Sep	Oct	Nov	Dec	Jan	Feb
Experian:																								
Equifax:	02	02	02	02	02	02	02	02	02	02	03	03	03	03	03	03	03	03	03	03	03	03	04	04
TransUnion:																				OK	OK	OK	OK	

We need this account to show up on Transunion and Experian. We should ask the others bureaus to include this account.

THE COMPLETE CREDIT CARE ™ PROGRAM

PF CU

	EXPERIAN	EQUIFAX	TRANSUNION
Account Name:		PFF FEDERAL	PLF CU
Account Number:		1XXXX	1XXXX
Acct Type:		Open Account	Installment account
Acct Status:			Open
Monthly Payment:			$290.00
Date Open:		12/1/2001	12/1/2001
Balance:		$0.00	
Terms:		298 s	48 Months
High Balance:		$11,959.00	$11,959.00
Limit:			
Past Due:			$0.00
Payment Status:		Pays account as agreed	Paid or paying as agreed
Comments:		PAID ACCOUNT / ZERO BALANCE AUTO	

24-Month Payment History — ? Legend

Date:	Jan	Feb	Mar	Apr	May	Jun	Jul	Aug	Sep	Oct	Nov	Dec	Jan	Feb	Mar	Apr	May	Jun	Jul	Aug	Sep	Oct	Nov	Dec
Experian: Equifax:	02	02	02	02	02	02	02	02	02	02	02	02	03	03	03	03	03	03	03	03	03	03	03	03
TransUnion:	OK	OK	OK	OK	OK	OK	OK	OK	OK	OK	OK	OK	OK	OK	OK	OK	OK	OK	30	OK	OK	OK	OK	OK

This past 30 day late entry was back in 03. Leave it for later. Note also when you're disputing late pay, make sure you ask to have the late pays corrected. Don't ask for a delete if the account is helping your credit score. Deleting a good account that's showing late pays will hurt you.

STAN MORRIS

PFF FEDERAL

	EXPERIAN	EQUIFAX	TRANSUNION
Account Name:		PFF FEDERAL	
Account Number:		004XXXX	
Acct Type:		Open Account	
Acct Status:			
Monthly Payment:			
Date Open:		3/1/2000	
Balance:		$0.00	
Terms:		99 s	
High Balance:		$2,151.00	
Limit:			
Past Due:			
Payment Status:		Pays account as agreed	
Comments:		PAID ACCOUNT / ZERO BALANCE LINE OF CREDIT	

24-Month Payment History   ? Legend

Date:	Jan	Feb	Mar	Apr	May	Jun	Jul	Aug	Sep	Oct	Nov	Dec	Jan	Feb	Mar	Apr	May	Jun	Jul	Aug	Sep	Oct	Nov	Dec
Experian:																								
Equifax:	02	02	02	02	02	02	02	02	02	02	02	02	03	03	03	03	03	03	03	03	03	03	03	03
TransUnion:	OK	OK	OK	OK	OK	OK	OK	OK	OK	OK	OK	OK	OK	OK	OK	OK	OK	OK	OK	OK	OK	OK	OK	OK

Here is another example of an item that needs to be reported by Transunion and Experian.

THE COMPLETE CREDIT CARE ™ PROGRAM

P B CU

	EXPERIAN	EQUIFAX	TRANSUNION
Account Name:		PB FEDERAL	PB CU
Account Number:		004XXXX	004XXXX
Acct Type:		Open Account	Installment account
Acct Status:			Closed
Monthly Payment:			$97.00
Date Open:		5/1/2000	5/1/2000
Balance:		$0.00	$0.00
Terms:			24 Months
High Balance:		$2,117.00	$2,117.00
Limit:			
Past Due:			$0.00
Payment Status:		Pays account as agreed	Paid or paying as agreed
Comments:		PAID ACCOUNT / ZERO BALANCE	

24-Month Payment History [? Legend]

Date:	Feb	Mar	Apr	May	Jun	Jul	Aug	Sep	Oct	Nov	Dec	Jan	Feb	Mar	Apr	May	Jun	Jul	Aug	Sep	Oct	Nov	Dec	Jan
Experian:																								
Equifax:	00	00	00	00	00	00	00	00	00	00	00	00	01	01	01	01	01	01	01	01	01	01	01	02
TransUnion:			OK	OK	OK	OK	OK	OK	OK	OK	OK	OK	OK	OK	OK	OK	OK	OK	OK	OK	OK	OK	OK	OK
																								OK

This is an 'Oldie But Goodie' because it establishes a credit history since 2000. And it's a 'paid as agreed.' This is an important account to have in the bureau.

STAN MORRIS

PBCU	EXPERIAN	EQUIFAX	TRANSUNION
Account Name:			PBCU
Account Number:			6XXXX
Acct Type:			Installment account
Acct Status:			Open
Monthly Payment:			$267.00
Date Open:			12/16/2005
Balance:			$3,707.00
Terms:			20 Months
High Balance:			$13,422.00
Limit:			
Past Due:			$0.00
Payment Status:			Paid or paying as agreed
Comments:			

24-Month Payment History   ? Legend

Date:	Feb	Mar	Apr	May	Jun	Jul	Aug	Sep	Oct	Nov	Dec	Jan	Feb	Mar	Apr	May	Jun	Jul	Aug	Sep	Oct	Nov	Dec	Jan
Experian																								
Equifax:	08	08	08	08	08	08	08	08	08	08	09	09	09	09	09	09	09	09	09	09	09	09	09	10
TransUnion:	OK	OK	OK	OK	OK	OK	OK	OK	OK	OK	OK	OK	OK	OK	OK	OK	OK	OK	30	30	OK	OK	OK	OK

The above account has 2 times past 30. This is an account that has to be fixed. These two times past 30 that's less than 2 years old will hurt a credit score badly. First call the creditor and ask if they would give you a pass on the bureau by changing the way they are reporting the account with two 30 days past. Especially if you've been a good customer for a while. They may do it for you. If they won't, just dispute it and see if you can get the late payments taken off. If the bureaus send you a letter saying they've been verified then re-dipute the item at least two more times before giving up. If they refuse to take it off then here is one time that I would write them a 100 word comment that is allowed by the bureaus explaining why the account is showing 2 times 30 late.

THE COMPLETE CREDIT CARE ™ PROGRAM

PBCU	EXPERIAN	EQUIFAX	TRANSUNION
Account Name:			PBCU
Account Number:			3001XXXX
Acct Type:			Overdraft / reserve checking account
Acct Status:			Open
Monthly Payment:			$109.00
Date Open:			11/14/2003
Balance:			$2,747.00
Terms:			Minimum
High Balance:			$3,007.00
Limit:			$3,007.00
Past Due:			$0.00
Payment Status:			Paid or paying as agreed
Comments:			

24-Month Payment History ? Legend

Date:	Feb	Mar	Apr	May	Jun	Jul	Aug	Sep	Oct	Nov	Dec	Jan	Feb	Mar	Apr	May	Jun	Jul	Aug	Sep	Oct	Nov	Dec	Jan
Experian:																								
Equifax:	08	08	08	08	08	08	08	08	08	08	08	09	09	09	09	09	09	09	09	09	09	09	09	10
TransUnion:	OK	OK	OK	OK	OK	OK	OK	OK	OK	OK	OK	OK	OK	OK	OK	OK	OK	OK	OK	OK	OK	OK	OK	OK

This is another great account but they need to be reported by the other bureaus.

STAN MORRIS

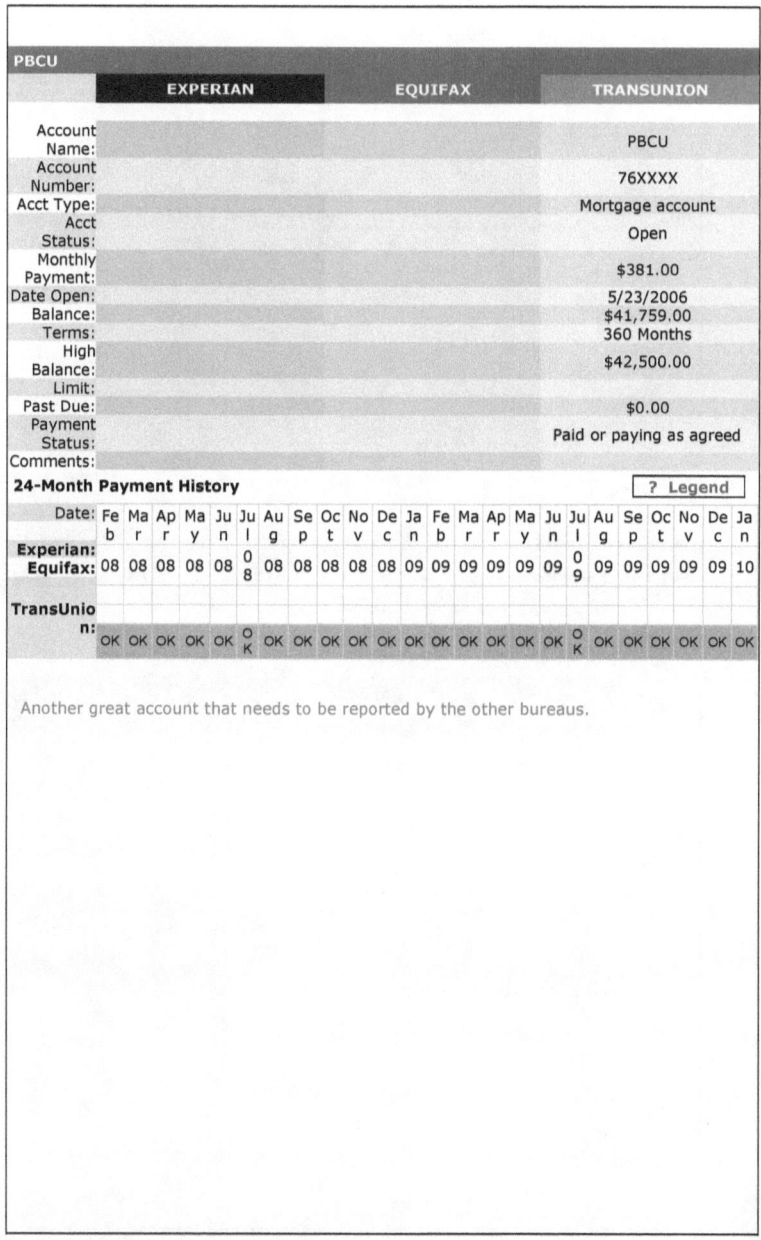

PBCU	EXPERIAN	EQUIFAX	TRANSUNION
Account Name:			PBCU
Account Number:			76XXXX
Acct Type:			Mortgage account
Acct Status:			Open
Monthly Payment:			$381.00
Date Open:			5/23/2006
Balance:			$41,759.00
Terms:			360 Months
High Balance:			$42,500.00
Limit:			
Past Due:			$0.00
Payment Status:			Paid or paying as agreed
Comments:			

24-Month Payment History   ? Legend

Date:	Feb	Mar	Apr	May	Jun	Jul	Aug	Sep	Oct	Nov	Dec	Jan	Feb	Mar	Apr	May	Jun	Jul	Aug	Sep	Oct	Nov	Dec	Jan
Experian:																								
Equifax:	08	08	08	08	08	08	08	08	08	08	08	09	09	09	09	09	09	09	09	09	09	09	09	10
TransUnion:	OK	OK	OK	OK	OK	OK	OK	OK	OK	OK	OK	OK	OK	OK	OK	OK	OK	OK	OK	OK	OK	OK	OK	OK

Another great account that needs to be reported by the other bureaus.

THE COMPLETE CREDIT CARE ™ PROGRAM

PORTRC	EXPERIAN	EQUIFAX	TRANSUNION
Account Name:	PORT	PORTREC	PORTRC
Account Number:	1xxxx	1xxxx	1xxxx
Acct Type:	Unknown - Credit Extension, Review, Or Collection	Open Account	Collection Account
Acct Status:	Closed	Closed	Closed
Monthly Payment:			
Date Open:	8/1/2007	8/1/2007	8/27/2007
Balance:	$487.00	$487.00	$487.00
Terms:	1 Month		
High Balance:		$487.00	
Limit:	$250	$250	$250
Past Due:	$487.00	$487.00	
Payment Status:	Seriously past due date / assigned to attorney, collection agency, or credit grantor's internal collection department	At least 120 days or more than four payments past due	Collection account
Comments:	Date Closed 9/1/2006	Date Closed 8/1/2006	Date closed 8/1/2006

24-Month Payment History ? Legend

Date:	Mar	Apr	May	Jun	Jul	Aug	Sep	Oct	Nov	Dec	Jan	Feb	Mar	Apr	May	Jun	Jul	Aug	Sep	Oct	Nov	Dec	Jan	Feb
Experian:																								
Equifax:	08	08	08	08	08	08	08	08	08	08	09	09	09	09	09	09	09	09	09	09	09	09	10	10
TransUnion:	KD	KD	KD	KD	KD	KD	KD	KD	KD	KD	KD	KD	KD	KD	KD	KD	KD	KD	KD	KD	KD	KD	KD	KD
	OK	OK	OK	OK	OK	OK	OK	OK	OK	OK	OK	OK	OK	OK	OK	OK	OK	OK	OK	OK	OK	OK	OK	OK

Dispute the Equifax because it's still showing a collection after 3 years. The statute of limitations is past. Just dispute it as another 'never done business with this company.' There are other things that can be disputed as well. Don't ever dispute more than one thing wrong at a time with each account you're disputing. Do you see the limit on the account is $250.00? The past due amount is $487.00. How can this be right? It's not. This is reason enough to write them a dispute. Another error is notice the date closed is before the date opened. This is a common error and will always win a dispute. The high balance is greater than the credit limit as well. These are the types of errors you will learn to look for. These type errors are on just about every credit report I've ever looked at. Remember FCRA says the report has to be accurate. This type error has to come off.

STAN MORRIS

TECO

	EXPERIAN	EQUIFAX	TRANSUNION
Account Name:	TEKCO	TECO	TECO
Account Number:	131XXXX	131XXXX	131XXXX
Acct Type:	Collection Department / Agency / Attorney	Collection Account	Collection Account
Acct Status:	Closed		Open
Monthly Payment:			
Date Open:	5/1/2007	5/1/2007	5/18/2007
Balance:	$185.00	$185.00	$185.00
Terms:	1 Month		
High Balance:			
Limit:			
Past Due:	$185.00		
Payment Status:	Seriously past due date / assigned to attorney, collection agency, or credit grantor's internal collection department	Unpaid	Collection account
Comments:		Unpaid	Placed for collection

24-Month Payment History   ? Legend

Date:	Mar	Apr	May	Jun	Jul	Aug	Sep	Oct	Nov	Dec	Jan	Feb	Mar	Apr	May	Jun	Jul	Aug	Sep	Oct	Nov	Dec	Jan	Feb
Experian:																								
Equifax:	08	08	08	08	08	08	08	08	08	08	09	09	09	09	09	09	09	09	09	09	09	09	10	10
TransUnion:	ND	ND	ND	ND	ND	ND	ND	ND	ND	ND	ND	ND	ND	ND	ND	KD	ND	KD	ND	ND	ND	KD	ND	KD

Here is an account that needs to be disputed because it is still showing open and the Experian is showing closed.

Below are keys to understanding the squares under each item reported.

Legend

- OK **Current**
- ND **No Data Provided***
- 30 **30 Days Late**
- 60 **60 Days Late**
- 90 **90 Days Late**
- 120 **120 Days Late**
- KD **Key Derogatory****
- RF **Repossession or Foreclosure**
- PP **Payment Plan**

THE COMPLETE CREDIT CARE ™ PROGRAM

*Sometimes the credit bureaus do not have information from a particular month on file.

PLUS Score℠ Report

A PLUS Score is a numerical representation of your credit worthiness. The majority of lenders use some sort of credit scoring model to help predict what kind of credit risk you may be. For each bureau's score and personalized analysis, click on the colored tabs below.

| EXPERIAN | EQUIFAX | TRANSUNION |

PLUS Score from Experian

This PLUS Score is based on information from your **Experian** credit report.
Your PLUS Score is calculated using the information in your credit report. Since information often differs among your three bureau reports, your PLUS Scores based on those reports will also vary.

Your PLUS Score is: **546** on a scale of 330 - 830.

Your Credit Category is:

| **Very Poor** | Poor | Fair | Good | Excellent |

Percentile: Your credit rating ranks higher than 5.78% of U.S. consumers.

PLUS Score Analysis   ? Help

About your PLUS Score:

Your PLUS Score is formulated using the information in your credit file. Your PLUS Score can range between 330 and 830, with a higher score indicating a lower risk. There are many scoring models used in the marketplace. The type of score used, and its associated risk levels, may vary from lender to lender. But regardless of what scoring model is used, they all have one purpose: to summarize your creditworthiness. Keep in mind that your score is just one factor used in the application process. Other factors, such as your annual salary and length of employment, may also be considered by lenders when you apply for a loan.

What your PLUS Score means:

Currently, factors in your credit file indicate that you may be viewed as a high credit risk by lenders. Your rates and terms are likely to be high, such as on an auto loan, requiring large down payments and costing you more in the long run.

What this means to you:

Credit scoring can help you understand your overall credit rating and help companies better understand how to serve you. Overall benefits of credit scoring have included faster credit approvals, reduction in human error and bias, consistency, and better terms and rates for American consumers through reduced costs and losses for lenders. While lenders may use different scoring models to determine how you score, and each major credit bureau has its own method for calculating credit scores, the scoring models have been fairly well standardized so that a score at one bureau is roughly equivalent to the same score at another.

What factors raise your PLUS Score:

- You have a good cushion of available credit between your current balance and your credit limits on all open trades. This has a positive affect on your credit score. This cushion shows lenders that you are unlikely to overextend yourself financially.

- The total balance on all your credit cards is relatively low compared to your total available credit limit. This has a positive impact on your credit score.

- Your credit report does not contain negative public records, such as a bankruptcy, lien, lawsuit or judgment filed within the last two years. This is having a positive impact on your credit score. Public record items may remain on your credit report for 7 to 15 years, depending on the item.

What factors lower your PLUS Score:

- Your payment history shows 1 or more payments that were late by 30 days or more. Late payments count negatively against your credit score. Negative information can stay on your credit report for up to 7 years for some items, up to 10 years for bankruptcies and 15 years for unpaid tax liens.

- Having low credit limits on your accounts and loans counts negatively against your credit score. Having a high amount of credit is a positive factor because it indicates to lenders that other creditors have trusted you by lending you money in the past. However, since your major credit card limits are generally low, lenders may think you dont have enough experience with high limits.

- Each time a potential lender or landlord pulls your credit report for review, an inquiry is placed on your file. Inquiries stay on your credit report for up to 2 years. Having several inquiries on your credit report is negatively affecting your score. They are not necessarily negative information, but too many inquiries may indicate to lenders that you are trying to take on more new debt or possibly overextending yourself.

Consumer Statement:

Statement: No Statement(s) present at this time

DISCLAIMER

The PLUS Score[SM], developed by Experian, is not an endorsement or guarantee of your credit worthiness as seen by lenders. The different risk levels presented here are for educational use only. Your PLUS Score can help you understand what factors impact your credit score.

Please be aware that there are many scoring models used in the marketplace, and each lender's scoring model has its own set of factors. How each lender weighs their chosen factors may vary, but the exact formula used to calculate your score is proprietary. In general, the higher your score, the better your chances are of obtaining favorable rates and terms.

Your PLUS Score was calculated using your actual data from your credit file on the day that you requested your report, making it comparable to most scoring models in the industry. Keep in mind however that other factors, such as length of employment and annual salary, are often taken into consideration by lenders when making decisions about you.

Also note that each bureau has its own set of data, resulting in a separate PLUS Score for each of your credit files.

THE COMPLETE CREDIT CARE ™ PROGRAM

PLUS Score from Equifax

This PLUS Score is based on information from your **Equifax** credit report.
Your PLUS Score is calculated using the information in your credit report. Since information often differs among your three bureau reports, your PLUS Scores based on those reports will also vary.

Your PLUS Score is: **548** on a scale of 330 - 830.

Your Credit Category is:

| Very Poor | Poor | Fair | Good | Excellent |

Percentile: Your credit rating ranks higher than 6.27% of U.S. consumers.

PLUS Score Analysis   ? Help

About your PLUS Score:

Your PLUS Score is formulated using the information in your credit file. Your PLUS Score can range between 330 and 830, with a higher score indicating a lower risk. There are many scoring models used in the marketplace. The type of score used, and its associated risk levels, may vary from lender to lender. But regardless of what scoring model is used, they all have one purpose: to summarize your creditworthiness. Keep in mind that your score is just one factor used in the application process. Other factors, such as your annual salary and length of employment, may also be considered by lenders when you apply for a loan.

What your PLUS Score means:

Currently, factors in your credit file indicate that you may be viewed as a high credit risk by lenders. Your rates and terms are likely to be high, such as on an auto loan, requiring large down payments and costing you more in the long run.

What this means to you:

Credit scoring can help you understand your overall credit rating and help companies better understand how to serve you. Overall benefits of credit scoring have included faster credit approvals, reduction in human error and bias, consistency, and better terms and rates for American consumers through reduced costs and losses for lenders. While lenders may use different scoring models to determine how you score, and each major credit bureau has its own method for calculating credit scores, the scoring models have been fairly well standardized so that a score at one bureau is roughly equivalent to the same score at another.

What factors raise your PLUS Score:

• You have a good cushion of available credit between your current balance and your credit limits on all open trades. This has a positive affect on your credit score. This cushion shows lenders that you are unlikely to overextend yourself financially.

• The total balance on all your credit cards is relatively low compared to your total available credit limit. This has a positive impact on your credit score.

• Your credit report does not contain negative public records, such as a bankruptcy, lien, lawsuit or judgment filed within the last two years. This is having a positive impact on your credit score. Public record items may remain on your credit report for 7 to 15 years, depending on the item.

What factors lower your PLUS Score:

• Your payment history shows 1 or more payments that were late by 30 days or more. Late payments count negatively against your credit score. Negative information can stay on your credit report for up to 7 years for some items, up to 10 years for bankruptcies and 15 years for unpaid tax liens.

- Having low credit limits on your accounts and loans counts negatively against your credit score. Having a high amount of credit is a positive factor because it indicates to lenders that other creditors have trusted you by lending you money in the past. However, since your major credit card limits are generally low, lenders may think you dont have enough experience with high limits.

- Each time a potential lender or landlord pulls your credit report for review, an inquiry is placed on your file. Inquiries stay on your credit report for up to 2 years. Having several inquiries on your credit report is negatively affecting your score. They are not necessarily negative information, but too many inquiries may indicate to lenders that you are trying to take on more new debt or possibly overextending yourself.

DISCLAIMER

The PLUS Score[SM], developed by Experian, is not an endorsement or guarantee of your credit worthiness as seen by lenders. The different risk levels presented here are for educational use only. Your PLUS Score can help you understand what factors impact your credit score.

Please be aware that there are many scoring models used in the marketplace, and each lender's scoring model has its own set of factors. How each lender weighs their chosen factors may vary, but the exact formula used to calculate your score is proprietary. In general, the higher your score, the better your chances are of obtaining favorable rates and terms.

Your PLUS Score was calculated using your actual data from your credit file on the day that you requested your report, making it comparable to most scoring models in the industry. Keep in mind however that other factors, such as length of employment and annual salary, are often taken into consideration by lenders when making decisions about you.

Also note that each bureau has its own set of data, resulting in a separate PLUS Score for each of your credit files.

THE COMPLETE CREDIT CARE™ PROGRAM

PLUS Score from TransUnion

This PLUS Score is based on information from your **TransUnion** credit report.
Your PLUS Score is calculated using the information in your credit report. Since information often differs among your three bureau reports, your PLUS Scores based on those reports will also vary.

Your PLUS Score is: 546 on a scale of 330 - 830.

Your Credit Category is:

Very Poor	Poor	Fair	Good	Excellent

Percentile: Your credit rating ranks higher than 5.78% of U.S. consumers.

PLUS Score Analysis   ? Help

About your PLUS Score:

Your PLUS Score is formulated using the information in your credit file. Your PLUS Score can range between 330 and 830, with a higher score indicating a lower risk. There are many scoring models used in the marketplace. The type of score used, and its associated risk levels, may vary from lender to lender. But regardless of what scoring model is used, they all have one purpose: to summarize your creditworthiness. Keep in mind that your score is just one factor used in the application process. Other factors, such as your annual salary and length of employment, may also be considered by lenders when you apply for a loan.

What your PLUS Score means:

Currently, factors in your credit file indicate that you may be viewed as a high credit risk by lenders. Your rates and terms are likely to be high, such as on an auto loan, requiring large down payments and costing you more in the long run.

What this means to you:

Credit scoring can help you understand your overall credit rating and help companies better understand how to serve you. Overall benefits of credit scoring have included faster credit approvals, reduction in human error and bias, consistency, and better terms and rates for American consumers through reduced costs and losses for lenders. While lenders may use different scoring models to determine how you score, and each major credit bureau has its own method for calculating credit scores, the scoring models have been fairly well standardized so that a score at one bureau is roughly equivalent to the same score at another.

What factors raise your PLUS Score:

• You have at least 2 or more open major credit cards, such as Discover, American Express, VISA, or MasterCard, on your credit report. This often tells lenders that you are a responsible borrower and they may be more likely to see you as a good credit risk and extend you credit.

• Your credit file shows no record of any current delinquencies on real estate accounts, such as a mortgage. Having real estate accounts in good standing is viewed positively by lenders.

• Your credit report does not contain negative public records, such as a bankruptcy, lien, lawsuit or judgment filed within the last two years. This is having a positive impact on your credit score. Public record items may remain on your credit report for 7 to 15 years, depending on the item.

What factors lower your PLUS Score:

- Your payment history shows 1 or more payments that were late by 30 days or more. Late payments count negatively against your credit score. Negative information can stay on your credit report for up to 7 years for some items, up to 10 years for bankruptcies and 15 years for unpaid tax liens.

- At least 1 or more of your accounts has a balance that is close to your credit limit, which may be lowering your score. When your balance is high, this can indicate to lenders that you are likely to overextend yourself.

- Your overall balances are close to your overall credit limits, which may be lowering your score. Having high credit limits shows lenders that you are responsible with your credit, but when your balances are also high, it can indicate to lenders that you are likely to overextend yourself.

- Each time a potential lender or landlord pulls your credit report for review, an inquiry is placed on your file. Inquiries stay on your credit report for up to 2 years. Having several inquiries on your credit report is negatively affecting your score. They are not necessarily negative information, but too many inquiries may indicate to lenders that you are trying to take on more new debt or possibly overextending yourself.

DISCLAIMER

The PLUS Score[SM], developed by Experian, is not an endorsement or guarantee of your credit worthiness as seen by lenders. The different risk levels presented here are for educational use only. Your PLUS Score can help you understand what factors impact your credit score.

Please be aware that there are many scoring models used in the marketplace, and each lender's scoring model has its own set of factors. How each lender weighs their chosen factors may vary, but the exact formula used to calculate your score is proprietary. In general, the higher your score, the better your chances are of obtaining favorable rates and terms.

Your PLUS Score was calculated using your actual data from your credit file on the day that you requested your report, making it comparable to most scoring models in the industry. Keep in mind however that other factors, such as length of employment and annual salary, are often taken into consideration by lenders when making decisions about you.

Also note that each bureau has its own set of data, resulting in a separate PLUS Score for each of your credit files.

Read the scores and what affects your score. This gives you clues as to where to start looking. When you find the items affecting your score start to work on fixing them by following the example in the previous tutorial. There are sample letters for just about any error you can imagine at the end of this book. Do not duplicate them word for word. Copy them and put them in your own words. The last thing we want is for you to get a letter saying that your dispute is frivolous because it was just like someone else's that was sent in after reading this book.

Look for collection accounts less than two years old. Look for duplicate accounts. I've seen a credit card company try to collect an account and then sell it to another collection agency and then that second company sell it to still another company. All three accounts hitting the persons credit adversely. This is illegal. It's up to you to sniff this out and get it corrected. Keep in mind CRAs may not see it your way the first time you dispute it but never give up. Keep disputing until you are convinced you can't get them to change what they are reporting. If all else fails and you have proof, there are sample letters to the BBB and FTC at the end of this book. If you want to really cause them a lot of extra work and you feel you haven't been fairly treated write these

THE COMPLETE CREDIT CARE ™ PROGRAM

organizations and I assure you that your dispute will be looked at differently. Make sure you have it right before you do this because, if you aren't, other disputes you try might just be a waste of time. I have seen this used and used successfully.

Important: If you have balances on credit cards, start reducing the balances to 30% of your credit limit. If you have a credit card with a $1,000 limit, your balance reported to the credit bureau should be $300 and under in order to have a excellent credit score. If you go over this amount it will affect what is called your **Utilization Rate**

The two major components that account for about 75% of the total credit score are payment history and present amounts owed compared to what your limits are. Payment history tells how well you have met your obligations over the years; the amount owed is a snapshot of your indebtedness right now. If your credit history is short, your current indebtedness can be the most important factor determining your credit score.

How FICO credit scorers determine whether you are living beyond your means is to compare the outstanding debt on each of your accounts with the maximum amount of debt that the credit grantor has set for you on that account (credit limit.) As mentioned above, this generates a set of "utilization rates" for each of your accounts.

The higher the utilization rates, the lower the FICO score.

Your credit report must have a mixture of accounts to have a good score. For example: You need at least 3 to 4 resolving accounts listed in your credit report. You also need active installment accounts, e.g. mortgage, car loan. If you have an inactive installment that's ok but for an optimum score, it's best that you have had an active installment within the last two years.

Do not close your credit cards accounts - this will affect your credit score. If you already have many credit cards, do not close the accounts because all the damage to your credit score has already been done. Just put the card up and don't use it except spending small amounts to keep the card active. Credit card companies will close an account if it has been inactive for 18 months. Also please note that you want deep credit roots (accounts over 5 years) this will definitely raise your score greatly. So you need old good accounts to get that high score.

Before you pay a collection account, negotiate to receive a letter of deletion.

Start to clean up items on your credit report that directly affect your score. All marks do not affect your score as much as items older than two years.

Try calling your creditors who are reporting a late payment in your file within the last 24 months and request a **good faith payment adjustment** to your account and remove the past 30 days payment. You will be surprised how politeness and persistence pay off, just for asking. You can remind them that you are a good customer and would appreciate them greatly.

STAN MORRIS

Here are the 3 CRA's numbers and addresses:

Equifax: 800-685-1111

Experian: 866-200-6020

TransUnion: 800-888-4214

Trans Union
P.O. Box 1000
Chester, PA 19022

Equifax
P.O. Box 740241
Atlanta, GA 30374-0241

Experian
P.O. Box 2104
Allen, TX 75013-2104

Important Notice: If you are attempting to improve your credit or repair it, keep in mind that the techniques in this book are designed for individuals who had past problems but are currently on their feet, financially. If you are currently experiencing problems paying your bills, the credit repair process will not work. You must be totally caught up on all your bills for at least three months before you can start repairing your credit report.

THE COMPLETE CREDIT CARE ™ PROGRAM

The Two Fold Approach Plan

From the very beginning I've advocated raising your score by deleting derogatory items and then adding positive items. One of the fastest ways to start is to remove any collections. Try to get the ones that are less than 2 years old deleted first. Many people have collections account in their credit report and most are very small. Unpaid utility or phone bill or unpaid medical bills and credit card balances are examples. Anything showing outstanding debt is important! An unpaid collection item on your credit report can hurt your credit score by 50 points or more. Simply call up those collection agencies that you owe and ask this question: "Do you delete credit entries if I pay it off?" Many of the collection agencies will gladly take off the bad mark if you pay what you owe. Naturally if you owe more than you can afford to pay this won't work. But you can set payments up and pay them off for delete as well. One thing that I've had some of my clients do is to buy down the debt. In other words if someone owes $100, make an offer to settle for $40.00 and a deletion. The collection company will counter offer at less than $100.00 (the original amount) and when it's paid they will delete the account from the record. Included in the sample letters is a letter that you fill out and send to the collection agency asking for deletion when the bill is paid. Once they sign it and send it back to you send them the agreed amount (money order) and watch as it falls from your record. If the collection agency doesn't follow through, send the letter to the CRAs yourself. Not all collection agencies will delete the items, but some will. This process takes about 60 days after the bill is paid to show up on your bureau. If it's an emergency then get the bill paid and ask the collection agency to fax the deletion to the bureaus. If they won't, then get a fax number and a live person from the bureau on the phone and fax it yourself.

NOTE*****Please don't worry about trying to get old closed collections, charge offs or old P&L's off your report. Don't try to get items that are over two years old (except Judgments and Bankruptcies) off just because they show some over 30 day's old items on your report.

NOTE***** A charge-off account will never turn into a good account. After 2 years it will not kill your score. It will ding your score, forever.

NOTE***** An account that had a late payment will show positive within 12-24 months. If it doesn't report positive in that amount of time, get it updated with a dispute letter.

NOTE***** A closed account with a late payment will be reported for 7-10 years from the closed date.

Ok Let's get started

Get on line and get your reports from www.creditchecktotal.com

The very first screen after you've answered all their proof of who you are will have a report number. Make sure you write it down. Every dispute letter needs to have this number on it.

Look at all 3 reports. Go to the bottom of each bureau on the report. There you will find clues of the items you need to concentrate on.

If after you look at your report and you don't recognize the accounts (even just 1) call one of the bureaus and place a fraud alert (The first 90 days is free) on your account. Collection agencies, credit card companies and other companies make mistakes as well and it could be that they have you charged with an account that is not yours. CRAs get a heads-up to pay a little more attention when there is a fraud alert on the account. It also makes it easier sometimes to get those accounts removed. I had one client place a fraud alert on his account and requested proof that all these collections were his and they all came off because there was no proof (contract signature) they were ever his.

A). Next Steps

    1) Go to the public records portion of the report. If there are any judgments or bankruptcies we'll deal with them first.
    2) If there are either one of these showing on your report and they are not yours then dispute them. There is sample letters included.
    3) If there are judgments or bankruptcies that are still showing 10 years after satisfied or dismissed they can be disputed as well.
    4) If there are judgments or bankruptcies that have any wrong dates, or no dates or a wrong anything reported, you can dispute these as well. Also after 2 years the courthouse puts the information on microfiche. Most of the time it takes a lot of digging to verify any public records. After two years one can ask for verification. If they can't verify the public record it goes away from your credit report.
    5) After public records issues have been addressed look at all collections under two years old.
    6) If there are differences among bureaus make a note of them.
    7) On the collection accounts look to see if there are dates that do not add up. If this is the case dispute the dates first. If this doesn't work and it gets verified, dispute other errors you see on another later dispute. If all else fails make them prove it's yours by denying you've ever done business with this collection agency. (You haven't.)
    8) Go to the sample letters and pull the one that best fits your dispute. Do not use it word for word. Put it into your words.
    9) Make a copy of your driver's license and social security number then attach it to your dispute letter. (This is a must.)

THE COMPLETE CREDIT CARE ™ PROGRAM

10) Send up to 6 items to each bureau at a time, no more.
11) Do not send the letter certified signature required. Send it so that you get notified when it's delivered. There is a difference. Sometimes CRAs will not sign for it, if you send it certified, signature required.
12) Wait for 45 days to receive the results back from the bureaus' investigation. Sometimes you won't hear anything back from one or two of the CRAs. If this happens there is a letter in this course to send them. It's called a 30 day follow-up.
13) Another stall tactic of CRAs is to send a frivolous dispute response to you. If you receive this type letter there is a response letter for this as well in the sample letters. CRAs know if they send these type letters out, chances are they'll never hear from you again. That's what they are counting on. Don't let them win. You have rights and they're counting on your not using them.
14) When you receive the investigation letters back from CRAs you'll see the results of their efforts. Some of your disputes will be deleted and some won't. The ones that aren't deleted will have reasons of VERIFIED or NEW INFORMATION. Make sure if they state they're verified, the date reflects it. If it still has old dates listed then hold their feet to the fire by asking for immediate deletion because they didn't do what they said they would do. The ones that are left can be re-disputed with another reason. If you don't have another reason re-dispute the item with the same reason but stronger language. In fact you can even call them on this and get it fixed over the phone. (Unless you can prove your dispute, never call them.)
15) If the other items on your first dispute aren't fixed, re-dispute them.
16) Look at your report again and see if you can find other negative items (less than 2 years old) and study them. See if all the data is present. If it's not, dispute the items as incomplete.
17) Next, look at your inquiries. Did you know that in order to have your credit pulled you must give them permission? Most companies pulling your credit won't be able to prove you've given them permission because most of the time you've never signed the proper documents giving them that permission. Every time you have your credit report pulled (other than for yourself like at creditchecktotal.com) your credit score will suffer, somewhat. So, if you have several check marks on this part of your report, dispute and re-dispute. Make them prove you have had your credit run. You could capture a lot of points on your report by having these items taken off.
18) Repossessions are next. These are a real pain. There are several customers that have had them successfully removed. It takes persistence. It will take several letters. If you've had more than one showing on your report then until you get them off you will have a hard time financing an automobile. They will stay on for 7 years after the write-off. If there is one still on there and it's been over 7 years then dispute it. If it's younger than 7 years

then start disputing errors first. Here is an area that it makes a difference between what the creditchecktotal.com score is and the Industry score that will be viewed by an auto lender. The industry score will be hit harder for the repossession causing your score to be much lower.

19) If you've had a bankruptcy it's important for you to study all those discharged items. If you reaffirmed any items, and are still paying for them, look doubly close at those items. I've seen customers that have reaffirmed items and the bureaus not report it accurately. One thing to look for, at the bottom of the account, is any red less than 2 years old reporting. If it is, it's not being reported accurately. It's showing that you are taking bankruptcy every month on this item. Dispute the item and your score will move 100 points, immediately. This is a common error I see every day. Look at the date. Look at the comments. If it shows in BK and there is a KD or any red at the history segment then there are problems. If it shows behind or late then dispute this. This is the kiss of death for credit scores. Don't ask for removals; just ask them to fix the error.

Disputing Creditors

Never dispute creditors directly.

For some reason, I've had clients who were sending direct disputes to creditors. This is not a good strategy. The only time to contact a creditor is to work out a pay for delete and negotiate a lesser payment amount and pay for delete. You lose your right to dispute the credit bureaus when you dispute directly to the creditor or collector.

Delinquent Accounts

It's difficult to get this done but it is possible. It comes down to your persistence once again. In order to get these removed you must first be totally caught up on your bills and have made at least 3 payments on time before you even attempt disputing these accounts. If you can afford to pay it off try to use the pay for delete strategy. Sometimes the creditor wants to keep your business and will negotiate your keeping the account open by deleting the information from your account for you.

Incorrect Payment History

I touched on this earlier but I will give it one more go.

Many times in the payment history section you will see yellow squares with the numbers 30, 60, 90 and 120. If you see more than one set of numbers (more than 1 month) with the same set of numbers, chances are the account has been aged. It will appear maybe as 3 months in a row that you were 60 days late, as an example. The date of healing starts the first day of delinquency. So if they write it off 240 days after your first problem they've held the account open too long. It is not legal for a company to report an account this way. One reason for aging is to collect more fees and make the amount due larger. Another reason is for bookkeeping reasons inside the company. The healing of a credit score cannot begin until the account is closed or satisfied in same manner on the report. If it's left open after 240 days then it puts you in a worse situation. So, dispute the item as being aged and, more times than not, it will go away.

THE COMPLETE CREDIT CARE ™ PROGRAM

P&L or Charged Off Accounts

When you still owe any company money over a period of time, they usually will write your account off. It is indicated with a P&L which means they've written it off their books as a bad debt expense. This account will appear as a Charge OFF account, or P&L, which means Profit and Loss. It is very difficult to have these accounts removed from your credit report, but not impossible. First you must look on your credit report and take notice to the last date this company reported you to the credit bureau. If the lender has reported to bureau within the last twelve months, your best bet is to directly deal with that company and negotiate some type of settlement. Something like a pay for delete will sometimes work. If the credit report shows it's been years since they reported on this account you might have a good chance of getting the account removed. Once you contact the bureaus they will give the creditor your address and they may start contacting you again. Each state has statute of limitations. Some states are 3 years and some are 5 years. Check your state to see what your state laws are.

Debt Collectors

Under the <u>Fair Debt Collection Practices Act:</u>

A *debt collector may not use any false, deceptive,* or *misleading representation or means in connection with the collection of any debt. Without limiting the general application of the foregoing, the following conduct* is *a violation of this section* (8) *Communicating* or *threatening to communicate to any person credit information which* is *known* or *which should be known to be false, including the failure to communicate that a disputed debt* is *disputed.*

What does this mean?

If you "dispute" a debt, the debt collector (collection agency or debt buyer) must show the account on the credit report as being "disputed" - normally this is shown as "consumer disputes this account". NOTE*****Only dispute with these companies directly after all else has failed.

You must send a certified letter (keeping a signed copy) stating you dispute a debt. Send it to the collection agency or the junk debt buyer. Some courts have held that the debt collector has no requirement to tell the credit reporting agency that the account is disputed unless the debt collector updates the account.

If you have disputed the account and then the collection agency or junk debt buyer updates the account a couple of months later without saying "disputed by consumer" - then this may very well be a strong FDCPA and state law violation. If you dispute a debt properly and the collector continues to report the debt as due and outstanding without noting the dispute on your credit report, talk to a lawyer to discuss your legal rights. Another less known tactic is to sue them in small claims court. I'll go into that later.

If No One will Play Ball Here Is another Way To Get Items Removed From Your Report!

One other avenue to resolve credit dispute is using the small claims court. You don't have to have a lawyer and you can do it yourself. If you've done all you can and still can't get the matter resolved take them to small claims court. You can file for a small amount of damages because of inaccurate reporting. It costs $35 in the county I live in. Make sure you have all your ducks in a row. Most times you'll win by default because if you sue for $1 or a small amount the creditor will not show up nor will the bureaus. If the bureau has been unwilling to show proof of how they verified the account or if the account is in error for other reasons we've discussed then it is worth the time. When you file the suit make sure to name the creditor and the credit bureau.

If You Want to get Your Disputes Noticed.

Hand-write your dispute letter instead of typing. The reason for this is that most credit repair companies are sending professionally typed letters to the credit bureau disputing everything. Credit bureaus dislike credit repair companies because they cause them to perform tasks without pay. That is why these techniques are not widely publicized. So, recently, the credit bureaus have been refusing to investigate disputes that are professionally typed. You can avoid this by handwriting your letter. Remember; if you have a dispute, don't let the credit bureaus frighten you by exercising your legal rights to dispute errors on your credit report.

If you feel a credit bureau has violated your rights, file a formal written complaint to The Federal Trade Commission (F.T.C.). The Fair Credit Reporting Act is enforced by this agency. Write or call their National Headquarters: Federal Trade Commission, 6th Street & Pennsylvania Ave. NW, Washington, D.C. 20580.

Authors Note. Earlier I gave you a scenario of how much it was costing to have errors on a credit report. I'll give you some more facts now. At the time of this writing over 61% of Americans are living from pay check to pay check. It was 43% in 2004. I proved to you that some people are spending as much as $1800 a month because of errors on their credit report. Maybe you're not one of those, maybe you're spending half that much a month. Could you use that extra cash every month? It's up to you to change this. I know it can be done because my score used to be in the high 400's. My score is almost 800 today. You can do it.

OK Let's add Some Good Credit

Any successful credit repair consists of two phases: 1) Removing the negative listings from your credit report and 2) Adding new, positive listings.

Since just a couple of negative listings will earn a rejection from most creditors, repair of your negative credit should be the first priority. After bankruptcy, for example, the credit report will show many negative listings including the bankruptcy filing, discharge and numerous "included in bankruptcy" listings. While removing a bankruptcy from your credit report is no easy proposition, it is possible and definitely worth the effort. It has to be over two years old before you'll have any luck. Here is my thinking. These items are going to be removed in 10 years anyway. It is your job to see if you can get them removed sooner than later. If they can't prove the bankruptcy then by the law it has to be removed. If it's not reported accurately then it has to be fixed or removed.

Automotive financing will typically allow some negative credit before credit repair, but with higher interest rates. Recently auto lenders seem to be loosening up a little. I expect them to tighten up in the near future however. The thing is this. Often, automobile industry lenders change who they will lend to. The bottom line is go ahead and get your credit fixed so you don't have to deal with it. Make sure you have enough income. Call your dealer and ask for F&I. Ask them what their minimum income requirements are. Ask them what score range they are having luck with at the present. Keep in mind the score you are looking at will be lower than the one they see. It could vary as much as 50 points if you have a previous repo.

Getting A Credit Card

Standard rate credit cards seem to be the most difficult to obtain when it comes to credit that still needs credit repair. Most standard rate cards will reject you immediately for any negative credit whatsoever. Yet, there are many credit cards that work with bad credit and help you to repair your credit. Some require deposits and others require a significant annual fee. Most have low credit limits. Keep in mind you have to start somewhere. Just get online and start researching.

Establishing New Credit

Please keep in mind that it's all about the credit score and a good one will determine if you can get that loan or credit card. Credit bureaus only judge you for what have done recently, within the last two years. What happened in the past is mainly in the past but can hurt your overall score.

To rebuild your credit totally, with great roots or accounts over 5 years can take five years. It doesn't mean that you can't get a great mortgage or loan with about two years of good credit, but to make your credit life much easier 5 years history

THE COMPLETE CREDIT CARE™ PROGRAM

is better.

If you are rebuilding your credit after bankruptcy or a negative paying history; you can do the following: Note, since credit bureaus rate what you have done recently, it is important to add new credit.

Do not; I repeat, DO NOT give up after you have gone through a bankruptcy or bad credit paying history. If you shut down all your cards or do not add good credit or just start paying everything in cash, it will still hurt you two years later. So, after devastating credit problems, take massive action to start rebuilding your credit instantly.

The single most cost effective and powerful tool for consumers to increase their high credit limit and decrease their debt to credit ratio, is the use of Sub-Prime Merchandise Cards. These types of cards report to one of more of the major credit bureaus.

To their dismay, despite their benefits, these are the most misunderstood cards in the credit industry. A large portion of the misunderstanding is due mostly to marketers misrepresenting the cards and the growing number of companies promoting them. When you learn how they work you'll understand why they have been the subject of much misrepresentation.

A Sub-Prime Merchandise Card is nothing more than a card attached to a line of credit which allows you to buy merchandise from a specific vendor (more than likely the company that sold you the card.) The merchandise will be purchased through a catalog or online mall. I can tell you that the merchandise is usually very expensive. Keep in mind why you are getting the card to begin with. It's to increase your credit score. These cards will do that. Make sure you have a card that is legit. I haven't seen any bad ones lately but I'm sure they are out there. Do your due-diligence before you sign up for one. Make sure it reports to at least one credit bureau. The other bureaus are supposed to pick it up if it doesn't you can get the other bureaus to pick it up by writing a dispute.

I'll give you a tip. If you have a parent or relative that has a good credit card account; ask them to put you on as a user. This doesn't mean you have a card and can carry it because they probably won't want you to do that. When you're put on a card as a user it is important that your address is the same as the card holder's address. It's really important also if your last name is the same. If it's not you won't get the full benefit however you will still get some points as long as the card holder stays in good standing. Be careful not to get into a situation whereby the cardholders account shows some late payments or charge-offs on the account because this will end up hurting your score more than improving it.

What If You've Never Had Any Credit?

If you are new to credit and wondered how you can get started, there are a few main steps to establishing your credit.

1. **Open a checking account.** If you don't have a checking account, potential lenders become very skeptical about the way you handle you financial affairs.

Let's face the truth, having a checking account says a lot about the way you handle money. It gives you credibility. Although most lenders never bother to check to see if you actually have an account, just having a source where potential lenders can check to verify your financial position gives you more clout with that institution.

2. **Open a savings account.** When potential lenders see a savings account on your credit application, it gives them a good feeling concerning the way you handle your financial affairs, regardless to how small of amount you have in your account. **Always show a savings account on your credit application.**

3. **Open a charge account with a department store.** These accounts are usually the easiest to get when you are new to credit. Try talking to a credit manager before applying for a department store card to find out your chances of getting the card. You must remember when trying to establish credit, not to apply for several companies at one time. If you are turned down, a negative inquiry will be listed in your credit report. The very first time you apply for credit to lenders who are members of the credit bureau, the information on your application is given to the credit bureau and a credit item will automatically be establish in your name. This is the humble beginning of your credit report. Protect it!

Try getting a loan from a finance company and stay away from payday loans. Finance companies are usually more receptive to individuals who are just getting started in credit. Most of these institutions have built their business on new comers into the credit world. The interest rate is a lot higher than a bank, but your chances of getting started are greater. It seems that every lender wants you to already have credit, but no one wants to be first. Be sure you talk with a banker first to see your chances of getting a loan from their bank before applying to a finance company.

Find a co-signer. Try to get your parents, relatives or a good friend to co-sign a loan for you.

THE COMPLETE CREDIT CARE ™ PROGRAM

Build Your Credit Using Current Bills.

PRBC connects people who lack a traditional credit history with lenders who want to reach them. They document and verify rental, utility, phone and other recurring payments that aren't reported to other credit bureaus.

http://www.prbc.com

Pay Rent, Build Credit, Inc. (PRBC) is an FCRA compliant credit repository that enables consumers and small business owners to build a credit line and credit score, based on their history of making rent and other recurring bill payments, that can be used to demonstrate creditworthiness when applying for housing, credit, insurance and employment.

Secured Credit Cards

When past credit rating is haunting you, it is best to create good credit to offset the bad. The goal is to establish new credit sources as quickly as possible and bury the bad among the good.

The best and easiest way to establish or re-establish your credit is through a secured credit card program. Many banks offer a secured MasterCard or Visa credit card to applicants regardless to past credit history. Applicants can qualify even if they never had credit before. You can obtain the card directly from the bank or through one of their agents for a transaction fee of about $35.00 -- which is well worth it.

NOTE*****This is not a debit card.

This is how the secured credit card program works. Applicants will open a savings account and deposit $250 to $500 with the bank that is issuing the credit card. The amount that is deposited will be slightly less or equal to the line of credit you will receive on the credit card and you can increase your limit as you wish, usually not exceeding $2500.00.

Another way to get a credit card is to go to Google and type-in secured credit cards. Make sure you get a Mastercard or Visa credit card. Do not get a debit card. Once you get the card use it. Never pay off the balance. Always pay off everything except $1. Here is what I've told many of my customers. Use the card and spend from it for things you would normally pay cash for gasoline, food, etc. The day you spend on the card put that cash in an envelope and hide it. Do not for any reason use that money for anything but to pay-down the credit card. When the bill is due take it and deposit it into the bank. Write your check and pay it off leaving only a one dollar balance. If someone feels like they have an emergency and they reach for your envelope "CUT OFF THEIR HANDS." Not really, but I wanted you to know how important it is to count that money as already gone. Never Never Never use it for anything other than paying off your credit card. If you own a credit card here is another simple rule. Never buy durable goods like cloths, TV's CD's etc on a credit card. Only use credit cards for things you would normally pay cash for and then put the cash up in a safe place. There is one time I do use my card other than I've just explained. When I see an item that I can buy and I'm sure I can sell it for more within a few days I'll use the card. I make sure I can sell it because that is what I'll use to pay off the card. I can build a little nest egg and make a little extra money when I do that as well. After you've had your secured card a few months the card company will give you an unsecured card. Then after you've had that card awhile and you've proved you can handle credit they will begin increasing your credit amount. Before long you'll begin receiving other credit card offers. The magic number is to try to have around $10,000 in credit limit with revolving credit cards. Remember to never use more than 30% of your limit on every card. 50% and over starts reducing your credit score.

THE COMPLETE CREDIT CARE™ PROGRAM

Sample Letters

On the next few pages you will find sample letters for you to use as a guideline in repairing or correcting your credit rating. You will notice that these preliminary letters are very short and directly to the point.

I've seen some clients receive great results when they made a copy of their credit reports and wrote the dispute directly on the copy and mailed it to the credit bureau.

Make sure you re-write the following sample letters to your style.

STAN MORRIS

Sample Letter: This Is Not My Account

Date

Name of Credit Bureau
Street Address of Credit Bureau
City State Zip
ATTN.: Consumer Relations Department

To Whom It May Concern:

I just received my credit report and there are some errors I need investigated. I noticed accounts and Inquires which do not belong to me.

Please remove these entries immediately.

AAA COMPANY NAME - ACCOUNT #

XXX COMPANY NAME - DATE OF INQUIRY

Please send me an updated copy of my credit report after you remove these entries. 30 days seems to be a reasonable time to complete this investigation.

Sincerely,

(signature)

Your Name
Your Social Security Number
Your Address
City State Zip

Send a copy of your Drivers Lic (with your current Address) or a copy of a utility or phone bill reflecting your address and a copy of your social security number. If you don't thy'll send it back to you.

THE COMPLETE CREDIT CARE ™ PROGRAM

If they respond back and tell you that they verified this account send this one back to them.

Name of Credit Bureau
Street Address of Credit Bureau
City State Zip
ATTN.: Consumer Relations Department

To Whom It May Concern:

I recently wrote you regarding account # (   ) I would like you to re-investigate this account. It is not mine. According to the FCRA you must make sure that the items you report on my credit file are accurate. Please provide me with copies of any invoices or contract where I signed for the goods. If you can't please delete this from my account. This account is not mine

Please remove these entries immediately.

AAA COMPANY NAME - ACCOUNT #

XXX COMPANY NAME - DATE OF INQUIRY

Please send me an updated copy of my credit report after you remove these entries. 30 days seems to be a reasonable time to complete this investigation.

Sincerely,

(signature)

Your Name
Your Social Security Number
Your Address
City State Zip

Send a copy of your Drivers Lic (with your current Address) or a copy of a utility or phone bill reflecting your address and a copy of your social security number. If you don't they'll send it back to you.

STAN MORRIS

If they still resist in correcting your report try it again. This time a little more stern.

Date

Name of Credit Bureau
Street Address of Credit Bureau
City State Zip
ATTN.: Consumer Relations Department

To Whom It May Concern:

I recently wrote you regarding account # (   ) I ask you to reinvestigate this account. You claimed you did but it is obvious you did not. You did not supply me with the names or copies of the contract that proves this is my account. You must remove this account from my credit report. I know my rights and I will follow through and write the FTC and the BBB if this isn't taken care of and I have proof from you that you took it off my record within 30 days.

Please remove these entries immediately.

ABC COMPANY NAME - ACCOUNT #

XYZ COMPANY NAME - DATE OF INQUIRY

Please send me an updated copy of my credit report after you remove these entries.

Sincerely,

(signature)

Your Name
Your Social Security Number
Your Address
City State Zip

Send a copy of your Drivers Lic (with your current Address) or a copy of a utility or phone bill reflecting your address and a copy of your social security number. If you don't they'll send it back to you.

THE COMPLETE CREDIT CARE ™ PROGRAM

**Sample Letter: If you have not heard
back from any bureau use a letter like this**

Date

Name of Credit Bureau
Street Address of Credit Bureau City State
Zip
ATTN.: Consumer Relations Department

To Whom It May Concern:

I recently wrote you regarding account # (   ) I ask you to
reinvestigate this account. As of today I have not heard back from
you. It has been over 45 days. According to the FCRA that is more
than ample time to handle my dispute. Since I haven't had a response
I can assume you have not been able to verify the account as it's
listed on my credit report. This means you must take it off. Please
send me the revised credit report showing this item has been
removed.

    ABC COMPANY NAME - ACCOUNT #

    XYZ COMPANY NAME - DATE OF INQUIRY

Sincerely,

(signature)

Your Name
Your Social Security Number Your Address
City State Zip

Send a copy of your Drivers Lic (with your current
Address) or a copy of a utility or phone bill reflecting
your address and a copy of your social security
number.

Sample Letter: I'm wondering Why Dispute Letter.

Date

Name of Credit Bureau
Street Address of Credit Bureau City State Zip
ATIN.: Consumer Relations Department

To Whom It May Concern

I'm wondering why you are reporting that I was late paying Company (account number). I'm disputing this. I am requesting that you take the late payments off this item and update my report to show the payments as paid as agreed.

The way you are reporting this account on my record is hurting my credit rating.

30 days seems to be a reasonable time to complete this investigation.

Sincerely,

(Signature)

Your Name
Your Social Security Number Your Address
City State Zip

Send a copy of your Drivers Lic (with your current Address) or a copy of a utility or phone bill reflecting your address and a copy of your social security number.

THE COMPLETE CREDIT CARE ™ PROGRAM

**Sample Letter: Incorrect Payment History
(Only used to get an entire account deleted)**

Date

Name of Credit Bureau
Street Address of Credit Bureau City State Zip
ATIN.: Consumer Relations Department

To Whom It may Concern:

I am in dispute of the following account.

Company, Acct. # --

This account was paid in full. Please delete this account from my report and forward me an updated copy of my credit report to reflect the changes.

30 days seems to be a reasonable time to complete this investigation.

Sincerely,

(Signature) Your Name
Your Social Security Number Your Address
City State Zip

Send a copy of your Drivers Lic (with your current Address) or a copy of a utility or phone bill reflecting your address and a copy of your social security number.

Sample Letter: Incorrect Payment History (only used to get a late payment entry deleted)

Date

Name of Credit Bureau
Street Address of Credit Bureau City State Zip
ATIN.: Consumer Relations Department

To Whom It may Concern:

I am in dispute of the following account.

Company, Acct. # --

I was never late paying this account. Please remove just the late payment history from my report and forward me an updated copy of my credit report to reflect the changes.

30 days seems to be a reasonable time to complete this investigation.

Sincerely,

(Signature) Your Name
Your Social Security Number Your Address
City State Zip

Send a copy of your Drivers Lic (with
your current Address) or a copy of a
utility or phone bill reflecting your
address and a copy of your social

THE COMPLETE CREDIT CARE ™ PROGRAM

Sample Letter: P&L Write Off

Name of Credit Bureau
Street Address of Credit Bureau City State Zip
ATTN.: Consumer Relations Department

Gentlemen:

I have never done business with this company before. I need you to verify that this is my account. Please include the name you contacted and how you verified this account to be mine. If you can't please delete it from my record immediately.

Company Account #

Please send me an updated copy of my credit report to show this deleted account. 30 days seems to be a reasonable time to complete this investigation.

Thank you for your cooperation.

Sincerely,

(Signature)

Your Name
Your Social Security Number

Your Address
City State Zip

Send a copy of your Drivers Lic (with your current Address) or a copy of a utility or phone bill reflecting your address and a copy of your social security number.

Sample Letter: Collection Accounts

Date

Name of Credit Bureau
Street Address of Credit Bureau City State Zip
ATTN.: Consumer Relations Department

To whom it may concern:

I have never done business with this company. Please send me proof where I have signed an invoice or contract with them. If you can't you must delete this account. Please send me a copy of my updated credit report after you take this off. 30 days seems to be a reasonable time to complete this investigation.

Your cooperation is greatly appreciated.

Sincerely,

(Signature)

Your Name
Your Social Security Number Your Address
City State Zip

Send a copy of your Drivers Lic (with
your current Address) or a copy of a
utility or phone bill reflecting your
address and a copy of your social
security number.

THE COMPLETE CREDIT CARE ™ PROGRAM

Sample Letter : Bankruptcy

Transunion Consumer Relations

P.O. Box 1000

Chester, PA 19022

August 7, 2010

Dear Transunion,

I have just received my credit report and have noted that it contains erroneous information regarding the following accounts. I would like them deleted from my record:

Creditor Name: CIRCUIT COURT -   Account #:xxxxx1 This account is listed as a Bankruptcy. Under provision 15 USC Section 1681i of the FCRA, I request that this item be verified and deleted from my record. (reason being……Wrong case number…..or wrong date…etc.) Example.I have never taken a bankruptcy on (date)..Please supply me with the method you used to verify this account, the persons name and address who supplied you with then information. If you can't please delete this account from my credit report.

Please investigate and delete these disputed items. 30 days constitutes a reasonable time to check these out. Please send an updated copy of my credit report to my (Present Address)

Your immediate attention to this matter is greatly appreciated. Please send me a copy of my updated credit report as soon as your investigation is complete.

Sincerely,

Name

Social Security Number: Birth Date:

Phone:

My present Address is :

STAN MORRIS

Sample Letter: Inquires

Date

Name of Credit Bureau
Street Address of Credit Bureau City State Zip
ATTN.: Consumer Relations Department

To whom it may concern:

I never authorized the following companies to check my credit rating. Please remove immediately.

AAA Company - Date of Inquiry

ZZZ Company - Date of Inquiry

Your cooperation in this matter is appreciated. 30 days seems to be a reasonable time to complete this investigation.

Sincerely,

(Signature)

Your Name
Your Social Security Number Your Address
City State Zip

Send a copy of your Drivers Lic (with your current Address) or a copy of a utility or phone bill reflecting your address and a copy of your social security number.

THE COMPLETE CREDIT CARE ™ PROGRAM

Sample Letter: Credit Bureau Reminder

Date

Name of Credit Bureau
Street Address of Credit Bureau City Sate
Zip

To whom it may concern:

Please refer to the letter I sent (Date), (please see enclosed copy), in which I challenged negative information listed on my credit report.

As the date above, I have not heard from you. It's been almost (Amount of weeks or months) with no response.

Please respond to my request immediately or I will be forced to exercise my rights by contacting the FTC, and BBB.

(Your Signature)
YourName

Your Social Security Number Your Address
City State Zip

Sample Letter: 2nd Credit Bureau Reminder

Date

Name of Credit Bureau
Street Address of Credit Bureau City State
Zip

Dear (Bureau Name),

On (date), I contacted your bureau by certified mail to dispute incorrect entries listed on my credit report. It is my understanding that you must send me the results of my dispute within a reasonable time; however, as of the above date, I have not received a response from you.

Please delete the incorrect information I have disputed and send me an updated copy of my credit report. Also, please include the names and addresses of the companies or individuals who were directly checked with in regards to this matter.

Your cooperation is greatly appreciated.

Sincerely,
(Signature) Your
Name
Your Social Security Number Your
Address
City State Zip

THE COMPLETE CREDIT CARE ™ PROGRAM

Sample Letter: 3rd Credit Bureau Reminder

Name of Credit Bureau
Street Address of Credit Bureau City State Zip
ATIN.: Consumer Relations Department

Dear (Bureau Name),

I disputed information that you included in my credit report in a letter dated (date). I've enclosed a copy. I understand that under the FCRA I am entitled a response with a certain amount of days from you. As of today I have not received any response at all from your bureau. Please be advised I must receive a copy of the changes you've made within (15 business days) from receipt of this letter or I have the right to take legal actions under the FCRA. If I decide to take further actions I will seek damages for loss of credit and mental anguish because of your inactions.

Because of your violation of the FCRA time frame rules it's safe to assume that the information I have disputed has been corrected and all the negative data has been removed from my credit report.

Thank you for your kind attention to this matter and hope to receive my updated credit report soon.

Sincerely,
(Signature)
Your Name
Your Address
Your Social Security Number
Date

Sample Letter: Estoppel By Slience - Validation of Debt
(A letter to a Creditor or Collection Agency)

Name
Address
Date
Account ID
Dear Collection Agency,

This certified letter, receipt number#   is to formally advise you that I believe your company has violated several of my consumer rights. Specifically you:

- Failed to validate a debt at my request- FDCPA violation
- Continued to report a disputed debt to the CRA- FCRA violation

Not only have you ignored my prior requests for validation of debt (proof enclosed- receipt copies or letter copies) but you continue to report this debt to the credit bureaus causing damage to my character. This letter will again request that you follow the FDCPA and provide the following:

Validation of Debt Request

- Proof of your right to collect this alleged debt
- Balance claimed including all fees, interest and penalties
- Contract bearing my personal signature

As you may be aware, "Estoppel by Silence" legally means that you had a duty to speak but failed to do so therefore, that must mean you agree with me that this debt is false. I will use the Estoppel in my defense.

I expect to receive proof requested above, within 15 days of this letter. Should you again ignore my request for validation of debt I reserve the right to sue your company for violations of my consumer rights as indicated under both the FDCPA and the FCRA. I may seek damages from you if warranted.

Sincerely,

Your Name

THE COMPLETE CREDIT CARE ™ PROGRAM

Sample Letter: Negotiation: Collection Agency Or Creditor

Date

Person Name
Their Company Name
Address
City, State, & Zip

RE: Account Number Amount Owed

To whom it may concern:

This letter is to inform you that 1 received your letter dated (Date), (please see enclosed copy) stating that my proposal Dated (Date), (please see enclosed copy) was unacceptable.

It is my desire that this account be satisfied. Therefore, I am prepared to make a counter offer concerning my account. If 1 pay the balance of this account in full, will you then accept my proposal of deleting the negative mark off my consumer credit report? I am trying to make a new life for my family and I and would greatly appreciate you doing this if you decide to.

Please reconsider my offer. Thank you for everything.

Sincerely,

Your Name Your
Address
Your City, State, & Zip

STAN MORRIS

Sample Letter: Stop Collection Procedures
CEASE & DESIST

Date

Person Name
Their Company Name Address
City, State, & Zip

RE: Account Number

Gentlemen:

Please be advised that I am exercising my rights under The Federal Fair Debt Collection Act to have all collection procedures **STOP** immediately.

It is my understanding that all letters, phones calls, etc., must **CEASE** immediately or I can file a claim against your organization for non-compliance.

It is my regret that it came to this. However, I must take appropriate action to cease our communication.

Sincerely,

Your Name Your Address
Your City, State, & Zip

THE COMPLETE CREDIT CARE ™ PROGRAM

Sample Letter: Never Done Business With This Company Before

Transunion Consumer Relations (Or Any of the bureaus)

P.O. Box 1000

Chester, PA 19022

August 7, 2010

Dear Transunion,

I have just received my credit report and have noted that it contains erroneous information regarding the following accounts. I would like them deleted from my record:

Creditor Name: Cnmer Adja - Account #: 37xxxx This account is listed as a collection. I have never done business with this company before. Please send me a copy of the contract or document proving I've done business with this company. If you can't please delete this account from my records.

Please investigate and delete these disputed items. 30 days constitutes a reasonable time to check these out. Please send an updated copy of my credit report to my (present address)

Your immediate attention to this matter is greatly appreciated. Please send me a copy of my updated credit report as soon as your investigation is complete.

Sincerely,

Name

Social Security Number: Birth Date:

Phone

Present Address;

Previous Address:

STAN MORRIS

Sample Letter: Inaccurate information. (high balance is more than limit or balance owed is more than credit limit)

Transunion Consumer Relations (Or Any of the bureaus)

P.O. Box 1000

Chester, PA 19022

August 7, 2010

Dear Transunion,

I have just received my credit report and have noted that it contains erroneous information regarding the following accounts. I would like them deleted from my record:

Creditor Name: Cnser Adjp - Account #: 37xxxx This account is listed as a collection. The information is wrong. The high balance is higher than the credit limit. (Or the balance is higher than the credit limit). This is impossible. No account can have more owed than the limit set by the creditor. According to the FCRA all the information has to be accurate on my credit report. This is not. Please delete this erroneous item immediately. Please investigate and delete these disputed items. 30 days constitutes a reasonable time to check these out. Please send an updated copy of my credit report to my (present address)

Your immediate attention to this matter is greatly appreciated. Please send me a copy of my updated credit report as soon as your investigation is complete.

Sincerely,

Name

Social Security Number: Birth Date:

Phone   Present Address;

Previous Address:

THE COMPLETE CREDIT CARE ™ PROGRAM

Sample Letter: Incomplete Data

Equifax Consumer Relations

P.O. Box 105873

Atlanta, GA 30348

August 7, 2010

To whom it may concern:

Based on a review of my credit report, I am requesting you to investigate the listed items below in accordance with the Fair Credit Reporting Act.

Creditor Name: HS - Account #: 41xxxx I have ask you to remove this account because the information is incomplete. According to the Fair Credit Reporting Act the information has to be correct. How can it be correct if information is missing. Please delete this account from my file.

Your immediate attention to this matter is greatly appreciated. Please send me a copy of my updated credit report to: (Present Address) as soon as your investigation is complete.

Sincerely,

name

Social Security Number:

Birth Date:

Phone

Present Address

Previous Address

STAN MORRIS

Sample Letter: Please add this account to my report

Transunion Consumer Relations (Or Any of the bureaus)

P.O. Box 1000

Chester, PA 19022

August 7, 2010

Dear Transunion,

I have just received my credit report and have noted that it contains important information regarding the following accounts. I would like this tiem added to my record:

Creditor Name: Some Bank - Account #: 7xxxx This account is listed with other Bureaus. Please include this account on your report like the other bureaus has. Your not reporting it has hurt my credit score. Please investigate and delete these disputed items. 30 days constitutes a reasonable time to check these out. Please send an updated copy of my credit report to my (present address)

Your immediate attention to this matter is greatly appreciated. Please send me a copy of my updated credit report as soon as your investigation is complete.

Sincerely,

Name

Social Security Number: Birth Date:

Phone

Present Address;

Previous Address:

THE COMPLETE CREDIT CARE ™ PROGRAM

Sample Letter: Charge-Off or P&L Write Off

Equifax Consumer Relations

P.O. Box 105873

Atlanta, GA 30348

August 7, 2010

Dear Equifax,

I have just received my credit report and have noted that it contains erroneous information regarding the following accounts. I would like them deleted from my record:

Creditor Name: Bank- Account# 5xxx4xxxx This account is listed as a charge off. Please delete this account from my file. It was paid off with GAP insurance. This account is being reported wrong. Please delete it from my file.

Please investigate and delete these disputed items. 30 days constitutes a reasonable time to check these out. Please send an updated copy of my credit report to my (Present address)

Your immediate attention to this matter is greatly appreciated. Please send me a copy of my updated credit report as soon as your investigation is complete.

Sincerely,

name

Social Security Number: Birth Date:

Phone

Present Address
Previous Address

STAN MORRIS

Sample Letter: Unknown Creditor, Late Payment And Collections
(Example of more than one dispute to one Bureau)

Equifax Consumer Relations

P.O. Box 105873

Atlanta, GA 30348

August 7, 2010

Dear Equifax,

I have just received my credit report and have noted that it contains erroneous information regarding the following accounts. I would like them deleted from my record:

Creditor Name: **Nul Credit Company** - Account #: 22091353xxxx This account shows late payments. It is incorrect. This account is paid as agreed and reflects that in payment status. Please correct the late payments to reflect payments were made on time.

Creditor Name: **K Of KS** - Account #: 101280873xxxx This account is listed as a collection. I have never done business with this company before. Please send me a copy of the contract or document proving I've done business with this company. If you can't please delete this account from my records.

Creditor Name: **UNKNOWN** - Account #: 40xxxx This account is listed as a collection. I have never done business with this company before. Please send me a copy of the contract or document proving I've done business with this company. If you can't please delete this account from my records.

Creditor Name: **AHF** - Account #: 12548xxxx This account shows late payments. It is incorrect. This account is paid as agreed and reflects that in payment status. Please correct the late payments to reflect payments were made on time.

Creditor Name: **C T CORP** - Account #: 11xxxx This account shows late payments. It is incorrect. This account is paid as agreed. Please correct the late payments to reflect payments were made on time.

THE COMPLETE CREDIT CARE ™ PROGRAM

Please investigate and delete these disputed items. 30 days constitutes a reasonable time to check these out. Please send an updated copy of my credit report to my Present Address

Your immediate attention to this matter is greatly appreciated. Please send me a copy of my updated credit report as soon as your investigation is complete.

Sincerely,

Name

Social Security Number: Birth Date:

Phone

Present Address
Previous Address

Sample Letter: Unrated

Transunion Consumer Relations

P.O. Box 1000

Chester, PA 19022

August 7, 2010

Dear Transunion,

I have just received my credit report and have noted that it contains erroneous information regarding the following accounts. I would like them deleted from my record:

Creditor Name: A Finance - Account #: 10xxxx This account is showing as unrated. It needs to show current like the other bureaus. The way you are reporting this is hurting my score. Please fix this error and put this account in good standing.

Please investigate and correct these disputed items. 30 days constitutes a reasonable time to check these out. Please send an updated copy of my credit report to 101 North Cherry, Somewhere, St. Zip

Your immediate attention to this matter is greatly appreciated. Please send me a copy of my updated credit report as soon as your investigation is complete.

Sincerely,

Name

Social Security Number: Birth Date:

Phone

Address:

Previous Address:

THE COMPLETE CREDIT CARE ™ PROGRAM

Sample Letter: Account showing closed by other bureaus

Transunion Consumer Relations (Or Any of the bureaus)

P.O. Box 1000

Chester, PA 19022

August 7, 2010

Dear Transunion,

I have just received my credit report and have noted that it contains erroneous information regarding the following accounts. I would like them deleted from my record:

Creditor Name: ACA Adj - Account #: 37xxxx This account is listed as an open account. It is reporting in error. This account was closed several months ago. Refer to (bureaus name) for proof. Please delete this account because it is reporting wrong and the FCRA prohibits this type error. Attached and circled is my proof.

Please investigate and delete these disputed items. 30 days constitutes a reasonable time to check these out. Please send an updated copy of my credit report to my (present address)

Your immediate attention to this matter is greatly appreciated. Please send me a copy of my updated credit report as soon as your investigation is complete.

Sincerely,

Name

Social Security Number: Birth Date:

Phone

Present Address;

Previous Address:

STAN MORRIS

Sample Letter: Duplicate Accounts

Transunion Consumer Relations

P.O. Box 1000

Chester, PA 19022

August 7, 2010

To whom it may concern:

Based on a review of my credit report, I am requesting you to investigate the listed items below in accordance with the Fair Credit Reporting Act.

Creditor Name: G/CP - Account #: 6xxxxxx This account is reported more than once on my credit report. Notice that all the amounts are the same. Also notice that all the account numbers are the same. Please investigate and delete this account from my credit report immediately.

Creditor Name: GCP - Account #: 3xxxxx This account is reported more than once on my credit report. Please investigate and delete this account from my credit report immediately.

These accounts are all the same. The way it's being reported is hurting my credit. Please delete these items immediately. 30 days should be long enough to complete this request.

Your immediate attention to this matter is greatly appreciated. Please send me a copy of my updated credit report to: Route 4 Box? Elnore, HO 9xxxx as soon as your investigation is complete.

Sincerely,

Name

Social Security Number:

Birth Date:

Phone

Address

Previous address

THE COMPLETE CREDIT CARE™ PROGRAM

Sample Letter: Fraud Alert Sample

Equifax Consumer Relations

P.O. Box 105873

Atlanta, GA 30348

August 7, 2010

Dear Equifax,

I have just received my credit report and have noted that it contains erroneous information regarding the following accounts. I would like them deleted from my record:

Creditor Name: ARFINCL - Account #: 4xxxx This account is showing as mine. It is not. FRAUD ALERT......I have recently placed a fraud alert on my file. This is one of the reasons. Please verify this account as mine. You will find I have never signed any document giving this company the right to bill me for any services. Please delete this account from my record.

Creditor Name: NO-MEDC - Account #: 42xxxx This account is showing as mine. It is not. FRAUD ALERT......I have recently placed a fraud alert on my file. This is one of the reasons. Please verify this account as mine. You will find I have never signed any document giving this company the right to bill me for any services. Please delete this account from my record.

Creditor Name: CO-MECLR - Account #: 4xxxx This account is showing as mine. It is not. FRAUD ALERT......I have recently placed a fraud alert on my file. This is one of the reasons. Please verify this account as mine. You will find I have never signed any document giving this company the right to bill me for any services. Please delete this account from my record.

Creditor Name: NO-FIN5 - Account #: 43xxxx This account is showing as mine. It is not. FRAUD ALERT......I have recently placed a fraud alert on my file. This is one of the reasons. Please verify this account as mine. You will find I have never signed any document giving this company the right to bill me for any services. Please delete this account from my record.

Creditor Name: NC-MEDR - Account #: 56xxxx This account is showing as mine. It is not. FRAUD ALERT......I have recently placed a fraud alert on my file. This is one of the reasons. Please verify this

STAN MORRIS

account as mine. You will find I have never signed any document giving this company the right to bill me for any services. Please delete this account from my record.

Creditor Name: N-MER - Account #: 4xxxx This account is showing as mine. It is not. FRAUD ALERT......I have recently placed a fraud alert on my file. This is one of the reasons. Please verify this account as mine. You will find I have never signed any document giving this company the right to bill me for any services. Please delete this account from my record.

Creditor Name: NLR - Account #: 4892xxxx This account is showing as mine. It is not. FRAUD ALERT......I have recently placed a fraud alert on my file. This is one of the reasons. Please verify this account as mine. You will find I have never signed any document giving this company the right to bill me for any services. Please delete this account from my record.

Creditor Name: FRLIN CO - Account #: 19xxxx This account is showing as mine. It is not. FRAUD ALERT......I have recently placed a fraud alert on my file. This is one of the reasons. Please verify this account as mine. You will find I have never signed any document giving this company the right to bill me for any services. Please delete this account from my record.

Creditor Name: CG SERVICES - Account #: 8xxxx This account is showing as mine. It is not. FRAUD ALERT......I have recently placed a fraud alert on my file. This is one of the reasons. Please verify this account as mine. You will find I have never signed any document giving this company the right to bill me for any services. Please delete this account from my record.

Creditor Name: Unknown - Account #: 10xxxx This account is showing as mine. It is not. FRAUD ALERT......I have recently placed a fraud alert on my file. This is one of the reasons. Please verify this account as mine. You will find I have never signed any document giving this company the right to bill me for any services. Please delete this account from my record.

Please investigate and delete these disputed items. 30 days constitutes a reasonable time to check these out. Please send an updated copy of my credit report to my Present Address)

Your immediate attention to this matter is greatly appreciated. Please send me a copy of my updated credit report as soon as your investigation is complete.

Sincerely,

THE COMPLETE CREDIT CARE ™ PROGRAM

Name

Social Security Number: Birth Date:

Phone:

Present Address:
Previous Address:

STAN MORRIS

Sample Letter: Reconfirmed Bankruptcy Items Not Reporting Accurately

Experian Consumer Relations

P.O. Box 2002

Allen, TX 75013

August 7, 2010

To Whom it may concern:

Based on a review of my credit report, I am requesting you to investigate the listed items below in accordance with the Fair Credit Reporting Act.

Creditor Name: Ce USA - Account #: 41xxxx This account is reporting inaccurately. There is no way a bankruptcy should ever show late payment history. This is the second attempt that I have requested that you fix this item by deleting it. The FCRA states you must report items accurately. You are not please delete this item from my report.

Under provisions of the Fair Credit Reporting Act 15 U.S.C. Section 1681i, please reinvestigate and delete these disputed items. Thirty (30) days from receipt of this letter is the length of time you are allowed under 15 U.S.C. Section 1681i (5) (A) to complete these actions unless you notify me otherwise. It should be understood that failure to verify within this time constitutes non-verification, and the items must be promptly deleted according to Section 1681i (a).

Pursuant to 15 U.S.C. Section 1681i (d) of the Fair Credit Reporting Act, please notify me when the items have been deleted. Once this has been accomplished, please forward me an updated copy of my credit report to the address listed below. According to U.S.C. Section 1681j, there is no charge for notification of changes on my credit report.

Your immediate attention to this matter is greatly appreciated. Please send me a copy of my updated credit report to: (Present address) as soon as your investigation is complete.

Sincerely,

Name

Social Security Number: Birth Date:

Phone

Previous Address

Present Address

THE COMPLETE CREDIT CARE ™ PROGRAM

Sample Letter : Judgment

Transunion Consumer Relations

P.O. Box 1000

Chester, PA 19022

August 7, 2010

Dear Transunion,

I have just received my credit report and have noted that it contains erroneous information regarding the following accounts. I would like them deleted from my record:

Creditor Name: CIRCUIT COURT - Account #:xxxxx1 This account is listed as a judgment. Under provision 15 USC Section 1681i of the FCRA, I request that this item be verified and deleted from my record. Please supply me with the method you used to verify this account, the persons name and address who supplied you with then information. If you can't please delete this account from my credit report.

Creditor Name: CIRCUIT COURT - Account #: xxx This Account is listed wrong. It was included in the Bankruptcy that has been released. Please correct this error and delete it from my record.

Please investigate and delete these disputed items. 30 days constitutes a reasonable time to check these out. Please send an updated copy of my credit report to my (Present Address)

Your immediate attention to this matter is greatly appreciated. Please send me a copy of my updated credit report as soon as your investigation is complete.

Sincerely,

Name

Social Security Number: Birth Date:

Phone:

My present Address is :

Sample Letter: Repossession

Bureaus address

To Whom It May Concern:

I have just received my credit report and have noted that it contains erroneous information regarding the following accounts. I would like them investigated and deleted from my report:

Creditor Name: Ctance Accoc - Account #: 687 This account is listed as a repossession. This account should be removed because the debt is satisfied and therefore should not be reported as a repossession. Please delete this account from my credit report.

Please investigate and delete these disputed items. 30 days constitutes a reasonable time to check these out. Please send an updated copy of my credit report to my mailing address below.

Your immediate attention to this matter is greatly appreciated. Please send me a copy of my updated credit report as soon as your investigation is complete.

Sincerely,

Name
Mailing Address:

Social Security #:
Present Address:

Birthdate:
Previous Address:

THE COMPLETE CREDIT CARE ™ PROGRAM

Sample Letter: Response To Credit Bureau That Sent You A Frivolous Letter Back From A Dispute

4/16/2010

RE: Response to your frivolous and irrelevant letter

Dear Sir or Madam:

I am in receipt of your illegal letter claiming that my dispute is "frivolous and irrelevant."

You do not have the right, nor the authority to make this determination until you have done your job. Since you have not fulfilled your obligation under the law, and re-investigated my claims, you would see that they are not "frivolous and irrelevant"!

I have forwarded a copy of your refusal to assist me to the Federal Trade Commission and the subcommittee on Banking, Credit and Insurance.

I fully expect that you will fulfill your legal obligation and reinvestigate the items contained in my letter (enclosed again) and sent to you certified mail, return receipt requested.

Sincerely,

Name
Address

Social:
Birthdate:

STAN MORRIS

Sample Letter To The Federal Trade Commission Requesting Help Because A CRA Would Not Take Off A Derogatory Item.

Federal Trade Commission
6th & Pennsylvania Ave, NW.
Washington, DC 20580
4/16/2010

RE: Complaint to be filed against credit bureau

Dear Sir or Madam:

I understand that you have enforcement powers against credit bureaus under 15 U.S.C. § 1681s. Therefore, I wish to lodge a complaint with you so that you may be aware of and be able to act upon a matter of abuse of that Consumer Reporting Act.

Credit Bureau
Credit Bureau Address

This credit bureau has refused to comply with its obligations under the Fair Credit Reporting Act. The substance of my complaint is as follows:

Please investigate this matter and inform me of the results. The undersigned would be happy to furnish full particulars to you if you need further information for enforcement proceedings.

Sincerely,

Name
Address

Social:
Birthdate:

THE COMPLETE CREDIT CARE ™ PROGRAM

Sample Letter To The Better Business Bureau (Your State) Requesting Help Because A CRA Would Not Take Off A Derogatory Item.

BBB
Your State's Bureau Address

4/16/2010

RE: Complaint to be filed against credit bureau

Dear Sir or Madam:

I understand that you have enforcement powers against credit bureaus. Therefore, I wish to lodge a complaint with you so that you may be aware of and be able to act upon a matter of abuse of that Consumer Reporting Act.

Credit Bureau
Credit Bureau Address

This credit bureau has refused to comply with its obligations under the Fair Credit Reporting Act. The substance of my complaint is as follows:

Please investigate this matter and inform me of the results. The undersigned would be happy to furnish full particulars to you if you need further information for enforcement proceedings.

Sincerely,

Name
Address

Social:
Birthdate:

NOTE******* This same letter will work if you need to have a creditor investigated as well. I've had clients that had to send a letter to the BBB on banks because they were trying to keep other lenders from lending the client money at a better rate. The bank was reporting late pays and foreclosures that weren't accurate just to make a higher interest rate loan to my client and keep one of their competitors from giving them a look.

Sample Letter: If a bureau still reports collections during a dispute to collector or after a dispute to CRA has not yielded a response.

Credit Bureau ....

Re: failure to investigate my dispute

To Whom It May Concern:

As of today, I have not received a response from your organization regarding my dispute with (creditor and account number). This account is still being reported inaccurately.

Based on your action, you are in violation of the FCRA.

Please note the following case:

(Dornhecker roo Ameritech Cmp., 99 F. SUpp. 2d 918 (N.D. m. 2000).

A U.S. district court held that the Fair Credit Reporting Act (FCRA), 15 U.S.C. 1681 , permits consumers to bring private causes of action against furnishers of information to credit reporting agencies who fail to properly investigate disputed credit information.

With this information in mind, we can agree to settle this dispute by either of the following actions:

I: You can forward statutory damages of $1000 payable to me at once for your failure to investigate.

2: You can Fix the problem addressed,

(explain what you want.)

If you need to reach me, call me at (number)

Best Regards,

Your Name

Address

THE COMPLETE CREDIT CARE ™ PROGRAM

Track Your Success

The following section is designed to help you track your efforts. Each CRA has a section of its own. Look at each item on your credit report and determine the most pressing ones first. Write the name and account number on each CRA's page. It will be best to take one CRA at a time. After you've accomplished this write what you're going to dispute in the corresponding section to the right of the account number for the 1st dispute. Go to the calendar and count forward 45 days. If you haven't received any thing back from the CRA then fire them a letter called "A Reminder Letter", in the sample letter section. Mark your calendar for 15 days.
Keep following up with the appropriate letters as needed. Here is where they think you'll give up. If you receive a "Frivolous Letter" response from them, you have a sample letter for this as well. Keep in mind they will stall every way they can. DO NOT GIVE UP. This affects your financial future.

You'll notice there is room for each dispute to have up to three different letters for each item. If you dispute an item and you get an answer back that shows the item as verified or first look to see if the verified date is accurate. If it's been recently verified, re-dispute the item in stronger language or find another reason to dispute the item. Write the second letter to the bureau. Make sure you record the letter and the type of dispute and count 30 days forward so you'll know when the deadline is for them to respond.

This is a simple way to keep up with your efforts as you're improving your credit scores.

STAN MORRIS

EXPERIAN Dispute Record

Account Name:_____ Account Number:_____

Dispute Date:_____ Response Due Date:_____

1st Dispute Reason:_____

Experian Response Date:_____

Result:_____

2nd Dispute Date:_____ Response Due Date_____

2nd Dispute Reason:_____

Experian Response Date:_____

Result:_____

3rd Dispute Date:_____ Response Due Date:_____

3rd Dispute Reason:_____

Experian Response Date:_____

Other Actions and notes.

THE COMPLETE CREDIT CARE ™ PROGRAM

EXPERIAN Dispute Record

Account Name:_____ Account Number:_____

Dispute Date:_____ Response Due Date:_____

1st Dispute Reason:_____

Experian Response Date:_____

Result:_____

2nd Dispute Date:_____ Response Due Date_____

2nd Dispute Reason:_____

Experian Response Date:_____

Result:_____

3rd Dispute Date:_____ Response Due Date:_____

3rd Dispute Reason:_____

Experian Response Date:_____

Other Actions and notes.

STAN MORRIS

EXPERIAN Dispute Record

Account Name:_____ Account Number:_____

Dispute Date:_____ Response Due Date:_____

1st Dispute Reason:_____

Experian Response Date:_____

Result:_____

2nd Dispute Date:_____ Response Due Date_____

2nd Dispute Reason:_____

Experian Response Date:_____

Result:_____

3rd Dispute Date:_____ Response Due Date:_____

3rd Dispute Reason:_____

Experian Response Date:_____

Other Actions and notes._____

THE COMPLETE CREDIT CARE ™ PROGRAM

EXPERIAN Dispute Record

Account Name:_____ Account Number:_____

Dispute Date:_____ Response Due Date:_____

1st Dispute Reason:_____

Experian Response Date:_____

Result:_____

2nd Dispute Date:_____ Response Due Date_____

2nd Dispute Reason:_____

Experian Response Date:_____

Result:_____

3rd Dispute Date:_____ Response Due Date_____

3rd Dispute Reason:_____

Experian Response Date:_____

Other Actions and notes.

EXPERIAN Dispute Record

Account Name:_____ Account Number:_____

Dispute Date:_____ Response Due Date:_____

1st Dispute Reason:_____

Experian Response Date:_____

Result:_____

2nd Dispute Date:_____ Response Due Date_____

2nd Dispute Reason:_____

Experian Response Date:_____

Result:_____

3rd Dispute Date:_____ Response Due Date:_____

3rd Dispute Reason:_____

Experian Response Date:_____

Other Actions and notes.

THE COMPLETE CREDIT CARE™ PROGRAM

EXPERIAN Dispute Record

Account Name:_____ Account Number:_____

Dispute Date:_____ Response Due Date:_____

1st Dispute Reason:_____

Experian Response Date:_____

Result:_____

2nd Dispute Date:_____ Response Due Date_____

2nd Dispute Reason:_____

Experian Response Date:_____

Result:_____

3rd Dispute Date:_____ Response Due Date:_____

3rd Dispute Reason:_____

Experian Response Date:_____

Other Actions and notes.

STAN MORRIS

EXPERIAN Dispute Record

Account Name:_____ Account Number:_____

Dispute Date:_____ Response Due Date:_____

1st Dispute Reason:_____

Experian Response Date:_____

Result:_____

2nd Dispute Date:_____ Response Due Date_____

2nd Dispute Reason:_____

Experian Response Date:_____

Result:_____

3rd Dispute Date:_____ Response Due Date:_____

3rd Dispute Reason:_____

Experian Response Date:_____

Other Actions and notes._____

THE COMPLETE CREDIT CARE ™ PROGRAM

EXPERIAN Dispute Record

Account Name:_____ Account Number:_____

Dispute Date:_____ Response Due Date:_____

1st Dispute Reason:_____

Experian Response Date:_____

Result:_____

2nd Dispute Date:_____ Response Due Date_____

2nd Dispute Reason:_____

Experian Response Date:_____

Result:_____

3rd Dispute Date:_____ Response Due Date:_____

3rd Dispute Reason:_____

Experian Response Date:_____

Other Actions and notes._____

STAN MORRIS

EXPERIAN Dispute Record

Account Name:_____ Account Number:_____

Dispute Date:_____ Response Due Date:_____

1st Dispute Reason:_____

Experian Response Date:_____

Result:_____

2nd Dispute Date:_____ Response Due Date_____

2nd Dispute Reason:_____

Experian Response Date:_____

Result:_____

3rd Dispute Date:_____ Response Due Date:_____

3rd Dispute Reason:_____

Experian Response Date:_____

Other Actions and notes.

THE COMPLETE CREDIT CARE ™ PROGRAM

EXPERIAN Dispute Record

Account Name:_____ Account Number:_____

Dispute Date:_____ Response Due Date:_____

1st Dispute Reason:_____

Experian Response Date:_____

Result:_____

2nd Dispute Date:_____ Response Due Date_____

2nd Dispute Reason:_____

Experian Response Date:_____

Result:_____

3rd Dispute Date:_____ Response Due Date:_____

3rd Dispute Reason:_____

Experian Response Date:_____

Other Actions and notes._____

STAN MORRIS

EQUIFAX Dispute Record

Account Name:_____ Account Number:_____

Dispute Date:_____ Response Due Date:_____

1st Dispute Reason:_____

Experian Response Date:_____

Result:_____

2nd Dispute Date:_____ Response Due Date_____

2nd Dispute Reason:_____

Experian Response Date:_____

Result:_____

3rd Dispute Date:_____ Response Due Date:_____

3rd Dispute Reason:_____

Experian Response Date:_____

Other Actions and notes.

THE COMPLETE CREDIT CARE ™ PROGRAM

EQUIFAX Dispute Record

Account Name:_____ Account Number:_____

Dispute Date:_____ Response Due Date:_____

1st Dispute Reason:_____

Experian Response Date:_____

Result:_____

2nd Dispute Date:_____ Response Due Date_____

2nd Dispute Reason:_____

Experian Response Date:_____

Result:_____

3rd Dispute Date:_____ Response Due Date:_____

3rd Dispute Reason:_____

Experian Response Date:_____

Other Actions and notes.

STAN MORRIS

EQUIFAX Dispute Record

Account Name:_____ Account Number:_____

Dispute Date:_____ Response Due Date:_____

1st Dispute Reason:_____

Experian Response Date:_____

Result:_____

2nd Dispute Date:_____ Response Due Date_____

2nd Dispute Reason:_____

Experian Response Date:_____

Result:_____

3rd Dispute Date:_____ Response Due Date:_____

3rd Dispute Reason:_____

Experian Response Date:_____

Other Actions and notes.

THE COMPLETE CREDIT CARE™ PROGRAM

EQUIFAX Dispute Record

Account Name:_____ Account Number:_____

Dispute Date:_____ Response Due Date:_____

1st Dispute Reason:_____

Experian Response Date:_____

Result:_____

2nd Dispute Date:_____ Response Due Date_____

2nd Dispute Reason:_____

Experian Response Date:_____

Result:_____

3rd Dispute Date:_____ Response Due Date:_____

3rd Dispute Reason:_____

Experian Response Date:_____

Other Actions and notes.

STAN MORRIS

EQUIFAX Dispute Record

Account Name:_____ Account Number:_____

Dispute Date:_____ Response Due Date:_____

1st Dispute Reason:_____

Experian Response Date:_____

Result:_____

2nd Dispute Date:_____ Response Due Date_____

2nd Dispute Reason:_____

Experian Response Date:_____

Result:_____

3rd Dispute Date:_____ Response Due Date:_____

3rd Dispute Reason:_____

Experian Response Date:_____

Other Actions and notes.

THE COMPLETE CREDIT CARE ™ PROGRAM

EQUIFAX Dispute Record

Account Name:_____ Account Number:_____

Dispute Date:_____ Response Due Date:_____

1st Dispute Reason:_____

Experian Response Date:_____

Result:_____

2nd Dispute Date:_____ Response Due Date_____

2nd Dispute Reason:_____

Experian Response Date:_____

Result:_____

3rd Dispute Date:_____ Response Due Date:_____

3rd Dispute Reason:_____

Experian Response Date:_____

Other Actions and notes.

STAN MORRIS

EQUIFAX Dispute Record

Account Name:_____ Account Number:_____

Dispute Date:_____ Response Due Date:_____

1st Dispute Reason:_____

Experian Response Date:_____

Result:_____

2nd Dispute Date:_____ Response Due Date_____

2nd Dispute Reason:_____

Experian Response Date:_____

Result:_____

3rd Dispute Date:_____ Response Due Date:_____

3rd Dispute Reason:_____

Experian Response Date:_____

Other Actions and notes.

THE COMPLETE CREDIT CARE ™ PROGRAM

EQUIFAX Dispute Record

Account Name:_____ Account Number:_____

Dispute Date:_____ Response Due Date:_____

1st Dispute Reason:_____

Experian Response Date:_____

Result:_____

2nd Dispute Date:_____ Response Due Date_____

2nd Dispute Reason:_____

Experian Response Date:_____

Result:_____

3rd Dispute Date:_____ Response Due Date:_____

3rd Dispute Reason:_____

Experian Response Date:_____

Other Actions and notes.

EQUIFAX Dispute Record

Account Name:_____ Account Number:_____

Dispute Date:_____ Response Due Date:_____

1st Dispute Reason:_____

Experian Response Date:_____

Result:_____

2nd Dispute Date:_____ Response Due Date_____

2nd Dispute Reason:_____

Experian Response Date:_____

Result:_____

3rd Dispute Date:_____ Response Due Date:_____

3rd Dispute Reason:_____

Experian Response Date:_____

Other Actions and notes.

THE COMPLETE CREDIT CARE ™ PROGRAM

EQUIFAX Dispute Record

Account Name:_____ Account Number:_____

Dispute Date:_____ Response Due Date:_____

1st Dispute Reason:_____

Experian Response Date:_____

Result:_____

2nd Dispute Date:_____ Response Due Date_____

2nd Dispute Reason:_____

Experian Response Date:_____

Result:_____

3rd Dispute Date:_____ Response Due Date:_____

3rd Dispute Reason:_____

Experian Response Date:_____

Other Actions and notes.

STAN MORRIS

TRANSUNION Dispute Record

Account Name:_____ Account Number:_____

Dispute Date:_____ Response Due Date:_____

1st Dispute Reason:_____

Experian Response Date:_____

Result:_____

2nd Dispute Date:_____ Response Due Date_____

2nd Dispute Reason:_____

Experian Response Date:_____

Result:_____

3rd Dispute Date:_____ Response Due Date:_____

3rd Dispute Reason:_____

Experian Response Date:_____

Other Actions and notes.

THE COMPLETE CREDIT CARE ™ PROGRAM

TRANSUNION Dispute Record

Account Name:_____ Account Number:_____

Dispute Date:_____ Response Due Date:_____

1st Dispute Reason:_____

Experian Response Date:_____

Result:_____

2nd Dispute Date:_____ Response Due Date_____

2nd Dispute Reason:_____

Experian Response Date:_____

Result:_____

3rd Dispute Date:_____ Response Due Date:_____

3rd Dispute Reason:_____

Experian Response Date:_____

Other Actions and notes.

STAN MORRIS

TRANSUNION Dispute Record

Account Name:_____ Account Number:_____

Dispute Date:_____ Response Due Date:_____

1st Dispute Reason:_____

Experian Response Date:_____

Result:_____

2nd Dispute Date:_____ Response Due Date_____

2nd Dispute Reason:_____

Experian Response Date:_____

Result:_____

3rd Dispute Date:_____ Response Due Date:_____

3rd Dispute Reason:_____

Experian Response Date:_____

Other Actions and notes.

THE COMPLETE CREDIT CARE ™ PROGRAM

TRANSUNION Dispute Record

Account Name:_____ Account Number:_____

Dispute Date:_____ Response Due Date:_____

1st Dispute Reason:_____

Experian Response Date:_____

Result:_____

2nd Dispute Date:_____ Response Due Date_____

2nd Dispute Reason:_____

Experian Response Date:_____

Result:_____

3rd Dispute Date:_____ Response Due Date:_____

3rd Dispute Reason:_____

Experian Response Date:_____

Other Actions and notes.

STAN MORRIS

TRANSUNION Dispute Record

Account Name:_____ Account Number:_____

Dispute Date:_____ Response Due Date:_____

1st Dispute Reason:_____

Experian Response Date:_____

Result:_____

2nd Dispute Date:_____ Response Due Date_____

2nd Dispute Reason:_____

Experian Response Date:_____

Result:_____

3rd Dispute Date:_____ Response Due Date:_____

3rd Dispute Reason:_____

Experian Response Date:_____

Other Actions and notes.

THE COMPLETE CREDIT CARE ™ PROGRAM

TRANSUNION Dispute Record

Account Name:_____ Account Number:_____

Dispute Date:_____ Response Due Date:_____

1st Dispute Reason:_____

Experian Response Date:_____

Result:_____

2nd Dispute Date:_____ Response Due Date_____

2nd Dispute Reason:_____

Experian Response Date:_____

Result:_____

3rd Dispute Date:_____ Response Due Date:_____

3rd Dispute Reason:_____

Experian Response Date:_____

Other Actions and notes.

STAN MORRIS

TRANSUNION Dispute Record

Account Name:_____ Account Number:_____

Dispute Date:_____ Response Due Date:_____

1st Dispute Reason:_____

Experian Response Date:_____

Result:_____

2nd Dispute Date:_____ Response Due Date_____

2nd Dispute Reason:_____

Experian Response Date:_____

Result:_____

3rd Dispute Date:_____ Response Due Date:_____

3rd Dispute Reason:_____

Experian Response Date:_____

Other Actions and notes.

THE COMPLETE CREDIT CARE ™ PROGRAM

TRANSUNION Dispute Record

Account Name:_____ Account Number:_____

Dispute Date:_____ Response Due Date:_____

1st Dispute Reason:_____

Experian Response Date:_____

Result:_____

2nd Dispute Date:_____ Response Due Date_____

2nd Dispute Reason:_____

Experian Response Date:_____

Result:_____

3rd Dispute Date:_____ Response Due Date:_____

3rd Dispute Reason:_____

Experian Response Date:_____

Other Actions and notes.

STAN MORRIS

TRANSUNION Dispute Record

Account Name:_____ Account Number:_____

Dispute Date:_____ Response Due Date:_____

1st Dispute Reason:_____

Experian Response Date:_____

Result:_____

2nd Dispute Date:_____ Response Due Date_____

2nd Dispute Reason:_____

Experian Response Date:_____

Result:_____

3rd Dispute Date:_____ Response Due Date:_____

3rd Dispute Reason:_____

Experian Response Date:_____

Other Actions and notes.

THE COMPLETE CREDIT CARE ™ PROGRAM

TRANSUNION Dispute Record

Account Name:_____ Account Number:_____

Dispute Date:_____ Response Due Date:_____

1st Dispute Reason:_____

Experian Response Date:_____

Result:_____

2nd Dispute Date:_____ Response Due Date_____

2nd Dispute Reason:_____

Experian Response Date:_____

Result:_____

3rd Dispute Date:_____ Response Due Date:_____

3rd Dispute Reason:_____

Experian Response Date:_____

Other Actions and notes.

Good Luck! I hope this helps bring your credit scores up to a level that improves your standard of Living.

Stan Morris

www.ingramcontent.com/pod-product-compliance
Lightning Source LLC
LaVergne TN
LVHW091553060526
838200LV00036B/824